TRAIL-BLAZERS
OF
AMERICAN
ART

CARMENCITA *by* John Singer Sargent

TRAIL-BLAZERS
OF AMERICAN ART

By

GRACE IRWIN

KENNIKAT PRESS
Port Washington, N. Y./London

TRAIL-BLAZERS OF AMERICAN ART

Copyright, 1930, by Harper & Brothers
Reissued in 1971 by Kennikat Press by
arrangement with Harper & Row, Publishers, Inc.
Library of Congress Catalog Card No: 73-122875
ISBN 0-8046-1336-2

Manufactured by Taylor Publishing Company   Dallas, Texas

ESSAY AND GENERAL LITERATURE INDEX REPRINT SERIES

DEDICATED

TO

MY FATHER AND MOTHER

CONTENTS

ILLUSTRATIONS

TRAIL-BLAZERS
OF
AMERICAN
ART

GILBERT STUART

America's First Great Portrait Painter

HE STORY OF THOSE EARLY CO-
LONIAL DAYS IN NEW ENGLAND
IS NOT FILLED WITH GAYETY,
MUSIC, AND LAUGHTER, NOR
DID THE PIONEER NEW ENG-
landers own lovely clothes of bright and shining silks and
rich laces, nor were their homes filled with beautiful furniture and silverware or rare works of art! Those were grim,
stern days, and each day took great courage and a stout
heart to live it. We know that those New Englanders were
grave and solemn and we appreciate that they had much
to make them sober and serious. The early years, in a new
land—a land that is a vast forest, filled with savages
(although friendly at times, most often cruel and hostile)
—are years of bitter, hard struggling.

About two hundred years before these early settlers
were fighting their way in a New World, the great and
powerful Italian merchant princes had sent their ships to
all parts of the world (which were known to them) and
had brought back great wealth. Because they passionately
loved all that was beautiful, they used their wealth to make
their cities wonderful, with marvelous buildings, and they

encouraged the artists of their land to paint and to sculpture things of everlasting greatness. What a sad contrast were those Italian cities with those first little New England towns! And so we must not forget for one moment the heavy odds and the lack of wealth that our forefathers had to face. They were as bravely creating a new nation as those Italian artists were beautifully creating works of art.

Countries are always as proud of their writers, artists, and musicians as they are of their generals, statesmen, and inventors. Each in his own way adds to the glory of a nation's history. The stories of great artists are often filled with as much excitement, glamour, and can thrill one as much, as the tales of brave soldiers and sailors! The first story to be told of a great American artist is one of romance and high adventure. It is of Gilbert Stuart, who was born in this Colonial New England, two hundred years after Michelangelo, Raphael, and Leonardo da Vinci were born in Italy. These Italian artists lived in a wonderful period, and great noblemen, princes, kings, and popes patronized and favored them. There were splendid schools of art throughout Italy—the best, perhaps, the world has known. Then contrast this young artist in New England—and what he had about him! The first few American artists that there had been had gone away to England, and there were none to encourage him or to teach him. Besides, he was poor and his parents had no money to educate him in anything, much less art. Free schools were very few, and very, very different from the free schools of today. No

2

wonder Gilbert Stuart's life was rich in adventure and interest, for he had so many obstacles to overcome.

Gilbert Stuart's father came to this country from Scotland, and settled in Rhode Island near Newport. His name was also Gilbert Stuart, and back in Scotland he had been a brave and daring fighter. Perhaps his son inherited some of his father's wildness! The father had loved devotedly the young Scottish prince, "Charles Edward," who was affectionately called "Bonnie Prince Charlie," and had hoped to see him on the throne of Scotland. But this was not to be, for the young prince had to prove his right to the throne and had to fight for it. A prince who fights for a throne and does not win it is called "a Pretender." The young Pretender and his loyal followers were badly beaten at a place in Scotland called Culloden Moor, and among them was the first Gilbert Stuart. Very likely, he felt that those who had fought for the defeated prince would find it most uncomfortable under the rule of the victor, and so he decided to take himself out of Scotland, and we are very glad indeed that he made this wise decision and that his decision brought him to America.

By a strange coincidence, Bonnie Prince Charlie's last name was S-t-u-a-r-t, and before coming to America, Gilbert Stuart, the elder, had spelled his name S-t-e-w-a-r-t. Once away from Scotland, he decided to show his love and devotion to his prince, and so he made their names alike in spelling as well as in sound.

Gilbert Stuart's (the father of the artist) occupation in Rhode Island will seem very funny and strange to you. He had the first snuff-mill in America. *A snuff-mill!* In those days it was quite the thing, quite elegant, to take a pinch of snuff as one talked over the serious and weighty problems that confronted one on every side, as if to say, "Is this something worth sneezing about?" However popular snuff may have been, it does not seem to have been, as a business, a great financial success, for Stuart and his wife and three children had anything but an easy time.

Gilbert Stuart, America's first great portrait painter, was born in Narragansett County, Rhode Island, December 3, 1755, and he was the youngest of three children. The youngest and the wildest! His father was very good-natured and easy-going, and his mother was quite something of a beauty. He inherited, apparently, his mother's good looks and his father's good nature. It was often said that he was as good-looking as the royal Stuarts and very much like them. When his parents had him christened one long-ago Palm Sunday, they did not forget their devotion to Bonnie Prince Charlie, and called him "Charles Gilbert Stuart." Probably it made them happy to think they would have a "Bonnie Charlie Stuart" of their own. However, as he grew up he dropped the Charles, and he was always known as Gilbert Stuart.

Gilbert Stuart's early education was the best that poor parents could give a boy, in those days in America. There were schools, of course, and a few of the great colleges we know today had been started, but they were not for the poor. His devoted mother was ambitious that her son receive a good education and she certainly did the very best she could for him, even trying to teach him Latin, although she knew nothing about it. Teaching Latin doesn't seem at all easy, even if you are an excellent Latin scholar, but if you know nothing about it, one can only imagine that it must have been a sorry mess. His father arranged for him to go for a few years to a free school, supported by their church. He was not a good scholar at all, even though he was very bright and learned quickly, for he was always up to some mischief. Besides, he showed, very early, a great interest in one subject to the exclusion of all others, and that one was drawing. As a young boy he drew some excellent likenesses of the people about him. Probably this talent of his only distracted his teachers rather than cheered them.

What a contrast between then and now! A boy who longs to be an artist, even if he is poor, may go to a public school, have excellent drawing teachers, a lavish supply of beautiful papers, fine brushes, and paints! After school, he may wander about in department stores, or art shops, or, best of all, go to the museums filled with the world's greatest art treasures. He can find beautifully illustrated books in a library, or look over the colorful advertisements in the magazines. There is so much he may have—and there was so very little for the young artist back in those Colonial days. The wonder is that Gilbert Stuart persisted in wanting to paint, when he saw so little of it done about him. His future in America as an artist did not look very bright and brilliant. The artists in those days were content to paint signs, and as "high" as they might hope their art to get was over a tavern door, as a swinging sign to attract

5

travelers. As high as that and no higher! But Gilbert Stuart wanted to be an artist and nothing else; nothing could turn his attention from his ambition.

He very early showed one remarkable trait—a trait that showed throughout his life and which we will speak of again. He could draw a likeness of a person after he had not seen him for years! At eighteen he drew such a "speaking likeness" of his grandmother, that it brought tears to the eyes of his relatives—and she had been dead six years!

By a very lucky chance for Gilbert Stuart and all Americans to follow him, there was a young Scotch artist, Cosmo Alexander, traveling in this country for his health, so they say (although I can't imagine crossing the Atlantic Ocean in a small sailing-vessel for one's health). Gilbert Stuart heard of this young artist, and as he was visiting in Newport, he sought him out and showed him his drawings. Cosmo Alexander was very generous in his praise for the young Gilbert's work, and his generosity was also very practical, for he offered to give the boy drawing lessons. Gilbert was jubilant and he worked hard for two years with Alexander. At the end of that time Alexander longed for his native Scotland, and planned to go home—and take Gilbert with him. This to Gilbert was an opportunity almost beyond anything he had ever dreamed or hoped for! It was the first great adventure of his life. This was the first of four trips that Gilbert made across the Atlantic in a sailing-vessel. It is surprising the way he went back and forth in sailing-boats as unconcernedly as though they were huge ocean liners! It must have taken courage to cross the

6

ocean in those days, and if he had written a diary of those trips, it would have read like the most thrilling tale of adventures one could read. Every one of his trips was made with one thought uppermost in his mind—his painting.

That trip across to Scotland most certainly and unfortunately did not improve the health of Alexander, but might be said to have wrecked it completely, for he was back in Scotland but a short time when he realized that he had not long to live. Young Stuart's future, alone in a strange country, worried him, so he sent for a relative, who was also a painter, and begged him to look after the boy when he was dead. The relative promised, but fate stepped in in a most unhappy manner and prevented his keeping his promise! Alexander died first, and the relative very shortly after did exactly the same thing! It was a cruel and double blow to the boy, and it looked as though his high hopes that he had cherished on those long days across the Atlantic were to be completely dashed. It would have floored almost anyone being left so penniless and alone in a strange land, but not Gilbert Stuart. He hung on to his ambition with the grip of a bulldog! For two years he had a pretty awful time of it, and at last decided to go back to America for a while and see his own people again.

This second trip across the ocean must have been a heart-breaking one, and the days must have seemed endless and black, even when the sun was shining and the wind blowing the boat nearer and nearer to the distant shore. It wasn't even a first-rate sailing-boat—it was a coaling-vessel, and Gilbert Stuart was working his way, clothed in rags and tatters. None of the men on that boat were in the least interested in painting, you may be sure! Poor boy! What a bitter contrast with that trip over two years before under the care and protection of Cosmo Alexander.

When he got back to Narragansett County in Rhode Island, he found his old neighbors had something vastly more important to talk about than his pictures. Much had been happening since he went away, for it was in the year 1774, and a year before there had taken place the famous "Boston Tea Party," and all New England was still seething with excitement!

Gilbert Stuart would not speak of his years away; he shut his lips together, or changed the subject, when he was questioned. He wanted to forget them, to make believe they had never happened. Never in his lifetime could he be tempted into discussing them.

The Colonists were in a turmoil when he returned—a new nation was soon to be born. Gilbert Stuart must have been confused and bewildered at the change, and he could scarcely have realized how grave the situation was. He was hardly home again before he wished to be away. Nothing could take from him his interest in drawing. His years in Scotland had been unhappy years, but they had done one good thing for him—they had opened his eyes to good painting, for he had seen some fine work in Scotland, and it had spurred him on, with a renewed determination to succeed.

He was only a boy, and a born artist, and he could not appreciate the fact that people were intensely interested in

8

something other than his work and that they had no time to bother with him. And so we hear that he made his third trip across the Atlantic just before the Revolution. This time he went to England. He had no definite plans of what he was going to do, no money, and no friends, but he was filled with a stubborn hope that he must succeed in the end. People who feel that way usually do succeed.

When he arrived in England, he had to get work at once to earn a living. Besides Gilbert's love for painting, he was deeply fond of music and he could play an organ remarkably well. It was this gift for music that saved him from starving. He was weary and hungry one day, and wandering in the lovely English countryside, when he passed a church in which they were having a "try-out" for an organist. All the men and youths in the neighborhood who could play were trying their skill. Gilbert Stuart coolly walked himself in with the others, and to his joy and good fortune was chosen organist of the church! The salary he received was one that in these days we would consider ridiculously small, but to the young artist it was a neat fortune.

His mind, however, was not on music, but just where it had always been—on painting. But his music enabled him to get enough money together to go to London and begin the painting lessons that his heart desired.

Living in London at that time was an artist named Sir Benjamin West, who was an American, whose home had once been in Philadelphia. He is called the Dean of American painting, because he was America's first painter. Gilbert Stuart's story has been chosen because his fame has been greater and because his fame has lasted to this day, while Sir Benjamin West's work was more appreciated in the time in which he lived than it is today. That is why Gilbert Stuart is called America's first Great Portrait Painter—because his fame and name lived long after him. Sir Benjamin West was told that there was a young countryman of his in London, who was struggling to be an artist. Sir Benjamin West sent for the young American and he was very generous and very kind to him. He could not have been more so! He offered to give the boy lessons, and a home as well. He did everything within his power to help him, for which we admire and are grateful to him. Sir Benjamin knew all the popular and well-known artists in London, and he saw to it that Stuart met them as well. You have heard, no doubt, of at least one of these English artists —Romney, Gainsborough, and Sir Joshua Reynolds. Gilbert Stuart came to know them all well, and they received him like one of them.

His luck had changed, his faith in his future had been rewarded! He established a studio in London, and great people sought him and wanted to be painted by the brilliant young American, Gilbert Stuart. For years he had half starved, dressed sometimes in rags; but now he became celebrated for his elegance of dress, for he looked like a great beau and dandy. He was, as has been said, good-looking, and as he now dressed in the height of fashion, he was quite a personage to meet and to see! He lived for some time in great splendor, entertaining with royal hospitality.

Money rolled in on him, and he certainly knew how to spend it and to enjoy it!

He married a beauty, a Miss Charlotte Coates, and they together lived a very gay existence for a while. Perhaps you might think that all these pleasures and gayeties might have interfered with his painting? He was never serious as a man, but as a painter he always was. He was very conscientious, and painted always with the same pride in his work and the same sincere purpose that he had in the beginning.

Fashionable people liked to say that they had a picture painted by him, and to boast of it. But Gilbert Stuart was very independent, and he let no one patronize him, for he painted just whom he chose! He snubbed people right and left, treating those who thought themselves of great importance with insolent "cheek." While he was in London he painted many great nobles and three kings! People had to stand for his high-handed way of treating them, because he had become far too popular for them to scorn.

He would permit only six people to sit for him in one day, and he invented all sorts of clever schemes to keep the number down to six, for he could have painted many more had he wanted to! He painted hard all day, and entertained great nobles and lovely ladies in the evening. What a change from what he had known!

He took lessons from Sir Benjamin West, but he did not paint in the least like his teacher, nor in fact any of the other artists about him. His manner of painting was absolutely his own. He was his own master, and he taught himself, by just painting and painting and seeing things in his own way.

There are many interesting stories of those gay and brilliant London days—days in which Gilbert Stuart did very much as he pleased. He lived each day richly, for that day alone, with no thought or worry for the future. There is one funny story I shall tell you of this period in his life:

He always amused his sitters with gay and amusing stories. However, on one occasion his sitter grew restless and impatient and said:

"Sir, your stories are very entertaining, but do you realize that my time is precious? I feel uncomfortable."

"I am very glad of it," replied Stuart, coolly, "for I've felt so ever since you entered my studio."

"Why?" asked the other, in surprise.

"Because you look like a fool. Disarrange that fixed-up costume and I will get to work!" One can easily imagine how utterly foolish his sitter must have felt, to have come all "fussed up," thinking himself most attractive, and prepared to be condescending to the artist, and then to be told he looked like a fool!

You have heard many stories of Scotch thrift, but not one of them could apply to Gilbert Stuart. He inherited none of it from his Scotch ancestry. He flung money around heedlessly and recklessly. He never kept the slightest track of who owed him money or who it was to whom he owed money. He never made out bills, kept receipts or accounts of any kind. And of course this way of doing things must all mean that there is a day of reckoning ahead. It is very interesting that his friends loved him and were loyal to him in spite of this weakness; they probably felt that he was still something of a careless boy in this particular. They certainly had to come to his rescue many times and get him out of financial snarls. This trait of his may have been rather trying on his friends, but today it cannot mean much to us. In one way it has benefited all the people after him because he had to paint more and more pictures to keep up with his debts. It was hard luck for those about him, but it is rather good luck for us!

After he had been in London for several years he went to Dublin to live. There was some gossip about why he went to Dublin, and some say it was because he was financially embarrassed in London, wanted to get away, but perhaps the gossipers were mistaken, as they are most often, and it was his restless spirit that made him long for a change of scene!

The life in Dublin delighted him and he was very happy with the charming Irish gentlemen of the upper class he met, who had a great love for art and learning. Their dispositions were much like his own—gay, witty, hospitable, and with elegant manners. They loved him, as he loved them. He and his wife had five very interesting years in Dublin.

Gilbert Stuart did not learn any lessons in thrift in Dublin, and the good-natured Irish let him run up bills until at last he was in a pretty predicament. The only way he got out of his difficulty was painting the portrait of the warden of the debtors' prison, who was very fond of him. His friends arranged for him to go back to America, and to pay his way back and that of his wife, by painting a picture of the captain of the ship. So you see his tendency to get into debt did force him to paint more pictures for us to admire.

For a long time now he had been watching at a distance, and admiring the careers of, great Americans back in the land of his birth. He now understood what all that turmoil and excitement had meant back in 1774, when he first returned from Scotland. He had seen what happened, and the startling but wonderful changes back in America. But most of all he was awed and deeply impressed with the gallant and brave leader who had fought to bring this remarkable change about. He longed to paint a portrait of this distinguished American, longed as he never had to paint the great nobles and kings who had sat before him. He felt that if he were to paint this man he would bring his career to a glorious height.

He and his wife set sail for America in 1792, from Dublin. He arrived in America quite a different person from that ragged, half-starved boy who had worked his way once across the Atlantic in a coaling-vessel. Now he was a celebrated and popular artist at the summit of his career. The man he wished to paint was also at the height of his power—a man, too, who had once known what it was to be in tatters and half starved (one long and cruel winter), all for a cause he believed in with his whole heart. It was very fitting that these men should meet after they were victors in a long struggle.

Congress was in session in Philadelphia when Gilbert Stuart and his wife arrived in America. John Jay, chief justice of the United States, sent him with a letter of introduction to the man among all others in America whom he most wished to meet—President George Washington! The letter of introduction was really not at all necessary, for George Washington had heard, of course, of the brilliant artist and was looking forward to the meeting. The two distinguished Americans first met at a public reception, a meeting that is historic. I have mentioned the fact that Gilbert Stuart had a great deal of what we call "cheek," and that he was pretty insolent to almost everyone. And so, of course, we wonder how he is going to behave toward George Washington? For once in his life he was subdued, awed, silent, ill at ease, and very plainly impressed by the dignity of the great Washington. He showed that he was thinking, "You are a greater man than I," which was something he had never admitted to anyone before in his life.

Washington graciously and gladly agreed to sit for the artist. He had never had his portrait painted, and as there were no cameras in those days, there was no likeness of him at the time to be left for future Americans.

George Washington was very punctual when he came for his sittings, and very courteous, but Gilbert Stuart never felt natural and easy with him. The first portrait was not a success, for he could not use his usual method of entertaining his sitter with funny stories or jokes. There was something about this calm, serious face that made him feel that his usual chatter was out of place. Washington agreed to sit for another portrait, and this one was somewhat better, but even this one did not please Stuart. Washington did not want to sit for a third portrait—he rebelled, for a man who has been many years a daring and active soldier does not enjoy sitting very quiet and still, having his picture painted! It was Martha Washington, the President's wife, who persuaded him to sit that third time, and it is well she did, for it was the best of the three. Upon it hangs a tale! Mrs. Washington asked Gilbert Stuart to send it to her when it was finished, and he agreed. Stuart finished the head and part of the shoulders, and before going any further he began painting copies of it, until in all he is said to have made fifty copies of it and sold them. You may remember that it was said he could paint from memory some one he had not seen for years? This memory helped him as he painted from the copy. Of course, there were many people in the young United States who wished a painting of their President, and as there was no other way of reproducing a picture as there is today, each one had to be painted. After some years, Mrs. Washington asked for this third picture, and Gilbert Stuart bowed politely and answered, smoothly: "I promised to give it to you, madame, when it was finished, and you see it is not." He had had no intention of finishing it! You have all seen this portrait of Washington in your history book, or your school building, for it is the most popular of the many paintings of Washington.

In 1800, Thomas Jefferson, a French artist named L'Enfant, and George Washington made plans for the

GEORGE WASHINGTON *by* Gilbert Stuart

beautiful city of Washington, which was to be the nation's capital. Very soon after, Gilbert Stuart and his wife went there to live for several years. In these years he came to know and to paint men whose names were to go down in history, for there were Thomas Jefferson, Alexander Hamilton, James Madison, James Monroe, Benjamin Franklin, John Quincy Adams, and a gentleman from Boston named Paul Revere! Two ladies, also of whom you may have heard —Dolly Madison and Martha Washington? If you look in your history books, you may see some of these portraits reproduced—if not all, you will be sure to find at least three or four.

Gilbert Stuart painted the portraits of all the distinguished men—and their wives in many cases—who were the early leaders of this country. It is too bad that, with so great talent and with his great following, his last days were not free from worry; but he was always distressed about money, and then a new problem came to cause him more annoyance—inferior artists copied his work, and tried (and very often succeeded) passing it off as his. To think that he was paid $1,200 for his best picture of Washington, and not very long ago in New York City, Mr. Henry Frick paid $70,000 for it! Although Gilbert Stuart was harassed with money worries to the very end, this shows that the respect for his talent has grown steadily since his death.

However, he did have some happy hours those last years, for his countrymen enjoyed with a relish his funny stories, were amused at his use of snuff, and had a respect for his talent. He was respected and well-loved by his countrymen. To young and struggling artists he was always kind, encouraging, and generous, but to those who tried to "impress" him he always retained something of his old insolence. The husband of a very plain woman once complained haughtily that Gilbert Stuart's portrait of her was not "beautiful," and the artist retorted, coolly:

"What a business is this portrait painting! They bring me a potato, and expect me to paint a peach!"

Gilbert Stuart's portraits of Washington have made him known to every boy and girl in America, and many a young artist has copied, in his school days, the features of the great Washington, out of a history book, and in doing so has paid a compliment to the genius of Stuart and the greatness of Washington.

Mark Twain once said, "If George Washington were to arise from the dead and did not look like the Stuart portrait, the boys and girls of America would brand him an impostor!"

Gilbert Stuart is not to be remembered merely because he made "likenesses" of our early leaders, in a time when there were no cameras! Gilbert Stuart was a distinguished artist who painted beautifully in a manner all his own. His works belong not only in a history book to show how our first great men "looked," but they belong in the art museums along with the finest paintings done by American artists and those of other countries. And there, if you look, I am sure you will find them!

And so, in Boston, in 1828, America's first great portrait painter died, after a long and vividly interesting life, beloved and honored by his fellow countrymen. Gilbert Stuart's fame is secure, and he will always hold a distinguished place in the story of art in America!

II

GEORGE INNESS

America's Great Landscape Painter

N ONE SPRING DAY IN 1825—MAY DAY, TO BE EXACT—A BABY BOY WAS BORN IN A FARMHOUSE NEAR NEWBURGH ON THE HUDSON. IN ALL THE YEAR, THERE could not have been a more fitting day for this baby to have opened his eyes upon the world! Nature was at her loveliest and fairest, for the fields, forests, and hills were all soft greens again, after the bare, bleak browns of the long, hard winter. Tiny chicks were cracking their way into the sunshine, blossoms bursting into bloom, brooks were freed from their icy clutch and were babbling on their way once more, baby lambs and little calves were stretching out their long, wabbly, uncertain legs, curious to try their strength. George Inness, America's greatest landscape painter—painter of the out-of-doors—came into the world with the springtime, with its promise of everlasting life and beauty!

Only a few hundred miles away from this farmhouse on the Hudson, in which a father and mother were rejoicing in the birth of their fifth child, over in the city of Boston Gilbert Stuart was still painting the portraits that had made him famous, although now he was an old gentleman of seventy. George Inness was three years old before Gilbert Stuart died. How great had been the changes in this land since the day Stuart had been born! George Inness was born in Newburgh, in the State of New York, one of the original thirteen states of the United States of America. Gilbert Stuart had been born in the Colony of Rhode Island, which had belonged to Great Britain. A War of Independence had been fought and won, a new nation had been born, a Constitution written and accepted, and five Presidents had already stood at the head of the nation—Washington, John Adams, Jefferson, Monroe, Madison, and John Quincy Adams.

True indeed, there had been tremendous changes in this land, much had happened, much had been accomplished, but as far as art and artists were concerned there was little difference since the days of Gilbert Stuart's youth. This country had had little opportunity to think of either, for there had been too much of other things for them to do. Besides, there were still many people who believed, as the first Puritans did, that "art" was silly, vain, weak, and far too worldly! Their churches, as you know, were very bare and simple, and they never had a painting in them, or brilliant stained-glass windows! To "decorate and ornament" their churches or even themselves was to them sinful! Although George Inness was to have some advantages that Gilbert Stuart never had, they both knew what it meant in their youth to have neighbors, families, and countrymen as a whole, who were neither interested nor pleased in their desires to be artists!

George Inness's father was not poor like Gilbert Stuart's, for he inherited a great deal more thrift from his Scotch ancestors than had Stuart's! At the time in which they lived, George Inness's parents were considered prosperous, almost "rich." His father had been a very successful merchant and had managed to hold on to his money, so that at an early age he retired. He bought his farm at Newburgh, more for the pleasure of it, and the fact that it was a better place to bring up a big family of children (there were thirteen in all), than to make money. George was the last to be born on this farm, however, for when he was only a few months old his father decided to move to New York City. It was before the time of Hudson River steamboats, before the time of the "Hudson River Night Line and Day Line," and that trip down had to be made on some sort of an antiquated sailing-boat. George was very tenderly wrapped up, put into a basket, and carefully taken care of on that journey, so that he would be comfortable and safe.

After four years in the city, the family moved again, this time they went to Newark, New Jersey. Newark, at that period, was practically nothing but a little country town, and the Innesses' home was on the top of a high hill overlooking rich farm lands. It was not until later that these farm lands were laid out into streets. This "high hill" they lived on is now called High Street and it is in the very center of the city. It seems very strange to think of High Street, Newark, as ever having been a green hill overlooking farms, for today it is a long crowded street looking down on nothing but great department stores and factories, and the greenest thing on High Street now are the traffic lights with their flashing "go" signs to thousands of automobiles!

While George lived in Newark his father sent him to the Academy to school. He did not like school or studies, that was very evident (but of course all other boys do!). But, more unfortunate still, he did not make much progress. His father was utterly discouraged and was quite prepared to take him from school.

Besides not being studious, he delighted in mischievous pranks. He was an original youngster and clever, and some of his originality and cleverness he took out in inventing ways of teasing his brothers and sisters. He invented a galvanized battery, which *worked,* for he took much unholy joy in giving shocks to his sisters and brothers, and even the unfortunate family cat! He modeled snakes and toads and things that "girls are scared of" out of clay, very cleverly painted them so they looked real, and then had a great time frightening the maids in the house.

For all of this mischief, he was a dreamer of dreams—a child who lived in another world than his own. Very often this is so with delicate children, children who have not the robust health to go out and play with others; they content themselves with imagining something that gives them happiness. You see, George Inness had one handicap that Gilbert Stuart didn't—he was frail as a boy, and in fact almost all of his life was never very strong.

23

One day, when he was only a little fellow, he was wandering in the fields alone, and he came upon a man painting. George stood by and watched him, fascinated, delighted, and deeply thrilled. As the man looked over the landscape before him, and then put his brush upon the canvas, George longed to be doing the same thing. Something within him was stirred, and an ambition deep and lasting was born.

That very day, then and there, he made up his mind that when he grew up he would be a painter and he, too, would paint the hills, clouds, trees, fields, and sunsets. To him, no dream he had ever had was half as beautiful as this new one of his! He wished that he had a canvas as big and broad as the whole landscape itself, so that he could put into his picture all the beauty he saw and felt about him! This desire shows how big and broad were his dreams and his whole nature.

His parents were not, unfortunately, as happily impressed by this radiant daydream as was Inness himself. As a future, painting did not seem to them sane, sensible, or at all wonderful. This was the hardest thing George Inness had to bear as a child, harder even than his frail health. His parents could not, would not see anything for him but a trade of some kind. Oh, this has to be written in so many of the stories about artists, musicians, and inventors! It is almost always the first grim, hard battle they must fight—to be permitted to do the work dearest to their hearts.

Not only were his parents not impressed happily by his ambitions, but few of his neighbors would have been, either. As has been said before, America at that time had not a very high regard for artists. They had appreciated Gilbert Stuart in the end, but probably because they could see some use and sense to his painting—they showed how distinguished people about whom they were curious looked. He was as necessary as a photographer! Gilbert Stuart would not have considered this the greatest of compliments, for he felt himself to be an "artist" and not merely something mechanical. Alas for George Inness, there were few, if any, who could see any use whatsoever in painting "trees and fields."

America at this time had had few artists who had the courage to paint, for "artists" were not admired, in fact they were considered socially in the class with "play actors" or "circus performers," and long-haired, "half-starved poets," and so to have an "artist" in the family was more a disgrace than a thing to be proud of! It was certainly an unhappy outlook for the young, ambitious artist, and a tragic one. In France, at about this time, Jean François Millet, in his little country village, was delighting *his* neighbors, the humble, simple peasants about him, with his first drawings, and from their none too heavy purses they took what money they could possibly scrape together, and gave it to their young neighbor and sent him off to Paris with their savings and their blessings, love and good wishes! No such happy fate awaited George Inness!

Paint he *would,* whether his family wanted him to or no! He did have enough money to buy canvas and brushes.

We don't have to read, as the stories say of Benjamin West (you remember him as the teacher of Gilbert Stuart in London?), that he had to pull out the cat's whiskers and the fur on its tail to make paint brushes (and if you ask me, I don't believe this ever did happen, even if it *was* written a dozen times), George Inness had his materials and painted in oils even as a very young boy. He was painting, but he was not making money, as his brothers were; they were all doing very well in their various trades.

One day a lordly, smart young brother of his jibed at him, made fun of him because he hadn't earned any money. He jingled his coins in his pocket so they made as much noise as possible. Inness was no "sissy," as the boys of today would say; he promptly fell upon his brother and beat him up so thoroughly that the brother, quite humbled, made no further remarks on the contrast between them.

His father had given up hope by this time of making his son George a scholar, and had taken him out of school. He set him up in a grocery store, as the owner and proprietor (George was now fourteen). This store was at the corner of Washington and New streets, Newark. It was the regulation country grocery store of that time, selling everything, more or less. Oh yes, George agreed to manage it, but behind the counter he concealed a few paints, brushes, and an easel! There he would paint amid the herring boxes, onions, sulphur matches, pickles, needles, and pins, while he let his business wait. He had no care in the world about the future owner of a couple of salt herrings; his whole heart was in his painting. This new business venture of his lasted

one month, and then something of such great importance
happened that it changed the whole course of his life. It
was on a day that everybody about had wanted something
in his store (not to his pleasure, but to his annoyance), and
he was constantly interrupted in his painting. At the end
of the day, when he thought he might have had some
breathing-space and peace, a little girl entered the store.
George was down behind the counter, hoping to goodness,
if she could not find anyone to wait on her, that she would
get disgusted and take herself off. But not this little girl; she
stood up on her tiptoes and banged on the counter (probably she heard George moving behind it), and getting no
results from this banging, she pulled herself up higher and
leaned right over. George, infuriated, tried far beyond his
patience, sprang up like a jack-in-the-box and yelled at
her:

"What in the name of a thousand devils do—you—
want?"

The little girl fled, like Little Miss Moffatt from her
black spider, crying over her shoulder, as she went:

"Candles, candles, candles!"

"And that," thought George Inness to himself, darkly,
"is the end of my grocery career!" He stalked out of the
store, shut up tight the big wooden shutters, banged the
door and bolted it. With his beloved canvas over his arm,
he marched home. He had turned his back forever upon
any kind of commercial life, and his great career was begun!

His father gave up struggling against an ambition as
strong and determined as this, and with a shrug of resignation

27

decided that, since his son wanted to be a "good-for-nothing painter," he might as well let him have drawing-lessons. So he finally placed him in the studio of a man in Newark named Barber, the best to be had in the town. After a few short months, Barber declared that he could not teach George anything, for he knew as much as he did! For a very short time he worked in an engraver's office; but this work was tedious and did not give him much freedom to do as he wished, and so he gave it up.

None of his "lessons" were of much use or benefit to him. There was a French painter in New York who could boast he had studied in Paris, and because of this boast had built up quite a reputation for himself. George Inness studied with him for a short time. He learned a little about the handling of colors; but this teacher was not particularly good, and Inness soon left him.

When he was only a boy he married a young girl named Delia Miller, of Newark. She died soon after, and it was only an incident in his life, soon to be forgotten.

He had picked up at the studios and at the engraver's a few new ideas—enough to make him feel he now knew enough to open his own studio. But his opening of a studio of his own did not mean money—or recognition. There were among the landscape painters of the time very set rules—the foreground had to be painted just this way, the sky another. The artists who painted out-of-doors, set themselves down and painted exactly what they saw before them—each twig, each branch. As a good cook follows a recipe for cake, with two cups of this, a cup of that, and a dash of vanilla for flavoring, so those painters put into their pictures a few cups of sky, a few cups of ground, and a dash of trees for a flavoring! This makes a picture with no more soul feeling or beauty than a chocolate cake! George Inness could not paint this way—he had too much heart and soul, was too much of a genius; he would rather have starved; and that he might easily have done if for a while his brothers had not come to his rescue.

Corot, the great French landscape painter, knew, too, what it meant to have people not appreciate his paintings. They could not see why anyone wanted to put trees and fields in a picture. They were used to masterpieces of the great Italian painters, which were religious; they were used to the fine portrait paintings of the Dutch and Flemish painters; but they could not understand landscape painting. Corot, as well as Inness, had a very hard time selling his pictures.

Shortly after George Inness had established his own studio, he went one Sunday to church. It must be confessed that on this particular occasion the minister's well-planned sermon was utterly lost on him, for he had no ears for it! His eyes, not his ears, were serving him most happily. Across the aisle from him sat a lovely vision—a young and very charming girl. He watched her all through the service, and, for all of him, the minister might have talked all day, as long as this radiant creature listened to him— and he could sit and look at her! He romanced, as he sat spellbound, and had already decided that in the last chapter he and his fairy princess were married and lived happy ever after. When church was over, he followed her to her home. He waited until she was safely in the house, and then he promptly rang her door-bell. Oh, here she was again, this beautiful girl, and now facing him, looking up into his eyes. "Do you know where Miss Mary Inness lives?" he asked, most politely. Miss Mary Inness was his sister and he had just been talking to her a few minutes before! The young lady—Miss Elizabeth Hart—answered with equal politeness, that she had heard of "Miss Mary Inness," but "she did not live here." George had heard all he wanted—he knew the sound of her voice!

This, of course, was not the last time that he saw Miss Elizabeth Hart, by any means; but as "Miss Elizabeth Hart" he knew her only a very short time, for he knew her through forty-odd years as "Mrs. George Inness." Her family, of course, had been anything but pleased that their daughter wanted to marry a vagabond good-for-nothing artist; they would as soon have seen her married to a street singer. But contrary to all their gloomy prophecies, the marriage, in spite of ups and downs, was a supremely happy one throughout those long years. George Inness adored his lovely wife as few men can. She was everything in the world to him. She was a very wise woman, as well as a gentle one, and she took care of her husband as a devoted mother does of her little son. He was always like a young boy about some things, especially money, for he had neither any sense about it nor interest in it. He was generous to a fault; he would gladly have given away his last cent to help another.

His brothers, as I said before, had to come to his rescue; they bought his pictures when no one else would, and when they could they sold them. George Inness was like many artists—he could not ask people to buy his work; he was a very poor salesman. In fact, if a person made the slightest criticism or offered a suggestion about a painting, Inness would refuse absolutely to let him have it, even if he didn't know where his next dollar was coming from.

Not long after he was married he sat painting in the park one day, and of course, at such an unusual sight of a man painting in public, a crowd gathered. They stood and gazed at him, awed and curious, for a man performing a vastly puzzling trick could not have held their attention more! At last, one by one, the crowd melted silently away; but one man, more interested than the others, remained. When the painting was nearly finished he spoke for the first time: "If you bring that picture to my house when it is finished, I will give you one hundred dollars for it."

It was Ogden Haggerty who spoke, a prominent New York man. He was the first to recognize the genius of George Inness and the first to help him. He was so certain that he had been watching an artist who would some day become very great, that he offered to help him in every way he could. He felt that in America there was very little chance for an artist to get the inspiration or training he needed, so he offered to send Inness and his wife abroad to Italy for a few years; and so George Inness and his young wife set sail for Italy. The trip over on a sailing-vessel was a long and hard one; it took many tedious weeks.

He studied and painted very hard in Italy, and with all the eagerness of his passionate, intense nature. Above all, he liked to go to the haunts of the old masters—Titian, Raphael, Michelangelo—and fancy himself back in the days in which they had lived and worked. He tried, as he stood daydreaming, to imagine how they had felt; he wanted to feel their genius in himself.

After two years, he returned to America with his wife and two little daughters, to one of whom was given the name of Rosa Bonheur. Rosa Bonheur, as you know, was the celebrated painter of "The Horse Fair." After he had been home a short time, Mr. Haggerty sent him abroad again, this time to Paris. While he was in France he came to know some of the French landscape painters, chief of which was Corot. Although he was interested in them, he never at any time copied their way of working.

While he was in Paris this time (for he made several other trips abroad) his son George, Jr., was born. This boy of his was his most ardent admirer and longed to follow in his father's footsteps and become a celebrated artist. After George Inness was dead his son wrote a history of his father's life which makes very interesting reading, for it gives us a very true and fair picture of the great landscape painter.

When Inness returned to America he felt that he could begin his American career in great seriousness. He opened a studio in Brooklyn, New York, but, alas! his countrymen had not yet come to appreciate his work. For a while he had a desperately hard time keeping his head above water. In those days he was happy to receive a hundred dollars for a painting that in later years was to sell for thousands. He was so discouraged that he moved his family to Boston. Again his benefactor, Ogden Haggerty, came to his rescue. It was arranged that a prominent firm of picture dealers in Boston should take over the management of his paintings and sell them for him.

He brought his family to a home in a little suburb of Boston—Medfield. These years in Medfield were happier than any he had known up to this time. He was a tender, loving father to his children, eager to share their trials as well as joys. As he painted, his small son would sit close beside him, painting, too. And when Inness went out into the fields, up the hills or into the woodlands, his son was trudging at his heels. His boy took care of him just as lovingly as his wife, for he was very absent-minded, and his son carried along his best brushes, paint rags, and paints that he might forget.

He often went out into the woods and fields and simply studied it all, feeling the mystery of God in all about him. He believed God was in everything—the flaming sunset, the rain, and the green hills. This was his religion. This religious belief of his most likely gave his paintings so much of their feeling and beauty. He rarely painted right from nature; he did not sit down and paint just what was before him. For days he might sit quietly drinking in all the beauty of a scene, but he would go to his studio to paint it.

33

His studio at Medfield was, as his studios most often happened to be, a barn that had been made over; it was bare and plain. He was too much of a genius to believe that a studio fitted up with beautiful rugs and hangings made him paint any better.

Out-of-doors, he was quiet and serene, but when he began painting in his studio he was like a madman, for he was fired and swept away with the intensity of his feelings. He painted some very beautiful pictures in Medfield. One of them is called "Medfield Meadows."

Spring and summer months in Medfield were filled with joys and delights in spite of the great uncertainty about money. Winter, too, had its pleasures with its many happy hours skating on the Charles River, for there were few sports Inness loved more. And in the gay parties on the ice there was no better-looking, more distinguished figure than the artist himself. He wore a shawl skating, as nearly all men did in those days, and with his long black hair, and gay plaid shawl floating in the breeze, he was quite something to see!

Sometimes, in those days, he made a sale that brought him considerable money. On one such happy occasion he went to Boston and bought a diamond necklace for his beloved wife. When he got home he slipped the dazzling chain about her neck, very proud and happy he could give her such a gift. Some time later he remarked that she never wore it. Didn't she like it? "My dear," she answered, "I am saving it to wear with a silk or velvet dress; it does not

AUTUMN OAKS by George Inness

seem to be just the thing with calico!" But he insisted she wear it just once to please him. Then she had to admit the truth—she had sold it and put the money in the bank for him. He was deeply touched at her thoughtful care of him, and kissed her, saying, "You are the best wife in the world."

Those years in Medfield were the years of the Civil War; but much as Inness wanted to fight for his country, he was not permitted to do so—he was not strong enough. And so he made speeches, raised money, and did everything he could without going into battle. Shortly after the war he moved his family back to the state in which he had spent his childhood and where he was to spend the rest of his life—New Jersey. They went first to a little town near Perth Amboy, and the lovely scenery in northern New Jersey so fascinated him that he was happy and content to make his home in Montclair, New Jersey. There are many lovely and beautiful paintings that tell us of his love for the New Jersey hills, fields, and woodlands. Although fame and money came very slowly to him—for he was fifty before his work became known in his country—it came surely. As he struggled on through the years, his work grew steadily finer and more beautiful. At last, fame did come to him, and wealth as well, for in those last fifteen years of his life his income was twenty thousand dollars a year—a princely income in those days. But, as always, money did not interest him very much, and he worked for the love of what he was doing, more than riches!

There are some amusing tales of him after he became

famous. He cared little or nothing for fashions and dress. Once he was invited to a dinner party, to meet some very distinguished guests; the party was to be in his honor! His wife sent him off to New York with many instructions as to just what to wear and just how to behave (for all the world like a mother instructing her little boy!). He promised very sweetly and obediently to do exactly what he was told, and, to tell the truth, he meant to! The guests at the dinner party, eager to meet the now famous artist, waited and waited, and no George Inness appeared! At last they sat down at the table and told stories of absent-minded people they had known, and between mouthfuls they turned their eyes toward the door. Suddenly he dashed into the room, breathless, sputtering out apologies! He *had* forgotten everything—what he was to wear and the day and the hour of the banquet! He was in an old painting-jacket and his hair was touseled, but he was so sorry, so ashamed, so humble that he was freely forgiven. He proved in the end to be such a very interesting, charming guest, that those who had so patiently waited were delighted, and felt well paid for the long delay.

His paintings were now exhibited in many great cities, both here and in Europe, and the most powerful of art dealers bought them and sold them. He had kept faithful to all his first loves—the hills and woodlands, sunsets and misty rains—and his love for them had deepened and broadened, and so, of course, his art did as well. In spite of his long struggle to be known, his life was far from unhappy, because he did love his work so much and because

36

he had a wife that he adored. The fragrance of the woods, the glory of the sunset, and the devotion of beloved companions were dearer things to his heart than fame and money.

And that reminds us: Once when he was in a studio building looking for a friend—a fellow artist—he stumbled by chance into the studio of a stranger. The man took him for a poor old fellow looking for work as an artists' model (another time when he was not "dressed up"). "You've a fine head, my good man," the stranger said. "Undoubtedly you will get work if you go round to the various studios." Inness admitted he himself was an artist, and the stranger looked doubtful and asked if he ever had his work exhibited. Inness nodded, and when the man asked him where, he said: "Oh, wherever I can—New York, Chicago, Philadelphia, Boston, London, Paris, Berlin." The man stared at him in amazement, and when at last he heard Inness's name he exclaimed, "Not *George* Inness!" The man was altogether delighted, proud and happy to meet the famous artist.

It sometimes is said of Inness that he is "America's Corot," but this is not exactly fair. Inness never copied, and he was not at all a follower of Corot. He was, in many ways, as great a painter as Corot, and one of the greatest landscape painters in the history of art, regardless of country.

His health began to fail toward the end, and his wife took him abroad to Scotland for a rest. At first it seemed as though he were improving, and they were happy and

37

content. One summer evening in 1894 he stood spell-bound, deeply moved by the flaming glorious beauty of a sunset; sunsets always stirred him to his soul! "O God, how beautiful!" he breathed. These were his last words, for he fell back into the arms of her whom he loved best, the little princess of one long-ago Sunday in church!

III

WINSLOW HOMER

America's Great Marine Painter

OU WILL DISCOVER THAT THE STORIES OF AMERICAN ARTISTS ARE ALL VERY DIFFERENT— THAT THERE ARE FEW THAT ARE IN THE LEAST ALIKE. IN this book there are no two which are similar. In Europe there were great schools of art, or groups of artists who painted much the same way, painted much the same things, and with the same ideals and standards. In these groups there were always a few very outstanding and celebrated artists, but people could always tell, by looking at their paintings, to which "school" they belonged. Almost all of the great masters had their followers. Each American artist, however, has more or less worked out his own ideas, in his own way, and has followed no group or school, and when he died, no "schools" have sprung up to follow in his path. The American artist has been very independent and has worked according to his disposition and character. And certainly no artist was more independent, more American, than the one of whom I am about to write— Winslow Homer. Winslow Homer is our greatest marine painter, and as most boys and girls relish stories of the sea,

I am sure that they will find his story a most interesting one.

You remember, just before Thanksgiving, learning the words of that song which begins:

> The breaking waves dash high
> On a storm and rock-bound coast,
> And the woods against a stormy sky
> Their giant branches tossed?

It was upon this very stern and rock-bound coast (facing often a stormy sky) that Winslow Homer built his studio and painted in solitude for nearly thirty years! Some of his greatest paintings were done when

> The heavy night hung dark
> The hills and water o'er.

Boston, at the time Winslow Homer was born, in 1836, was a picturesque, snug little fishing-town. Its streets were narrow and crooked, running this way and that, making a regular network, as complicated as a fisherman's net! In this crisscross of crooked winding streets, lying between Faneuil Hall and Causeway Street, was the simple, modest home of Charles Savage Homer and his family. It was in this house that a second son, called Winslow, was born.

The Homer family were of good old New England stock, and a sturdy, long-lived one, for most of them reached the ripe old age of eighty-five years. The family had been in this country for two hundred years. An ancestor, Captain John Homer, sailed out of an English port in 1636, in his own boat, and so arrived in New England, not so many years after the first pilgrims.

Charles Savage Homer was a hardware merchant down in the section of Boston in which they lived. He himself was something of a character, for he inherited a great deal of daring and restlessness from the adventurous Captain John Homer. He was a handsome, dignified man, and would have made a fascinating hero for an exciting tale of adventure. Winslow liked to say, half in fun, when people were boasting of their families, that he had discovered that a grandfather of his was a pirate (a yarn pure and simple, because the grandfather to whom he referred was just a "Down East" storekeeper and as honest as the day was long). His father, however, went to look for gold and treasure, with those reckless adventurers of 1849—went to dig it from the ground, instead of murdering and stealing, as a pirate would. He sold out all his wares, jauntily decked himself out, and, with shining new brass-bound trunks, said good-by to his family one day in " '49." His boys were struck dumb with admiration, and very likely had large golden dreams of what was some day to be theirs. He had sent a sailing-vessel out of the port of Boston filled with mining machinery to go to California by way of Cape Horn and the Pacific Ocean! He planned to have it meet him, although he expected to reach California first, because he took the short way (which in those days was not "short" or easy). Two years later the gallant, gay, and hopeful Charles Savage Homer returned to his home, not covered or weighted down with gold, for nothing now glittered about him, not even the brass knobs on his trunk, for they were quite dull and his trunk was tied together with cords! Some one had jumped his claim and he was never able to win it back.

Mrs. Homer was a quiet, gentle little lady who had a pretty talent for painting flower pieces in water-colors. She was so interested in this work that she did quite an unusual thing for a married woman in those days—she continued taking lessons after the babies came. Many of her flower pieces have been piously preserved by her family.

The Homers moved from house to house about Boston— they had seven different homes in Winslow's early boyhood—some one (probably his father) had a roving spirit. One of their last homes was in Cambridge, on Main Street. It was a big, pleasant wooden house, and the boys had plenty of opportunities for all the fishing, boating, and swimming their hearts could have desired. Winslow always looked back upon this period of his life with pleasure, because of its joyous freedom. The beautiful surroundings made a deep impression upon him. Beauty and freedom were always very dear to him all the days of his life.

He and his brothers went to the Washington grammar-school in Cambridge. There were better free schools then than there had been in the days of Gilbert Stuart. Drawing was, of course, not taught, because it wasn't considered important, although in another twenty-five years the boys and girls of Boston *had* to take drawing as they did their reading and writing and arithmetic. In 1870, Boston made it a rule that drawing must be taught. It was the first city in the country to make such a ruling! But when Winslow was a boy there was very little real art work done in

America and there was not much done to encourage the young artists.

Winslow drew when he was a boy, and what was very remarkable, he never copied anything, but drew right from life. You know, this is not easy, for most boys and girls begin by copying pictures. Winslow Homer had one trait like Gilbert Stuart—he painted and drew extremely well from memory. When he was eleven, he made many sketches, and very carefully he signed each sketch and dated it. He put them away in perfect order, and kept them for years. He was, even as a boy, careful and serious. His companions at school remember him as a quiet boy with dark-brown eyes, with an honest, straightforward gaze. He did have plenty of fun in him, but it was not the boisterous, riotous kind. You have known people who have made you laugh in delight at something they have said in a very solemn fashion, without as much as blinking an eyelash? This was Winslow Homer's way—he had a keen sense of humor (for which we are thankful; it is easier to like people with a sense of humor). His humor is what we call "dry humor"; it is not the bubbling-over variety.

His father seems to have been a thoroughly understanding man, for he encouraged his son in his love of drawing. Once when he was in Paris (what a traveler that man was!) he sent home to Winslow a complete set of lithographs or prints showing heads, ears, noses, faces, houses, trees, and animals—just the kind of "studies" used by art students in Paris. This was a help to Winslow, for, although he loved drawing, it did not come easy to him; he had to work very hard at it, and practice was as necessary to him as "exercises" are to the musician. Drawing does not come easily, sometimes, even to the greatest artists; there is no royal road to success. Winslow realized that he must keep steadily at his work. He was a born artist, but, like the born musician, must keep working, working!

Perhaps he made some copies of these drawings in school. Many a boy makes drawings and cartoons when he is supposed to be studying—say geography, for instance! A big geography has protected many a young artist from his teacher's view! It always seems to be part of the history of young artists that "he covered his slate and the margins of his textbooks with sketches," although maybe he didn't at all, for he was a very serious, careful lad!

When he was only a boy of twelve he made some really remarkable drawings from life—he had his two brothers pose for him. "A Man with a Wheelbarrow," he called one of them, and it was very good indeed. Some of these drawings are very amusing.

When Winslow was nineteen his father thought of putting him to work in a haberdashery shop as a clerk. But, fortunately, before this happened he saw an advertisement asking for a boy to be apprenticed to a lithographer named "Bufford." The advertisement also requested that the boy have a talent for drawing. It was this last line which decided Winslow, and his father knew Bufford (they were members of the same volunteer fire department); he was given a two weeks' trial. One can't imagine any modern boy being at all delighted at the prospect of being apprenticed, for it meant working very hard for no money at all and with very little freedom, and added to this, three hundred dollars had to be paid for the privilege of learning the trade! Winslow Homer felt that this was an excellent chance for him, and that he could do no better than accept it.

Bufford soon discovered that Winslow Homer was extremely clever, and he did not demand that he be paid the usual three hundred dollars. If Winslow liked the actual work itself—making drawings on stone, from which other drawings could be printed—he hated the drudgery, routine, and lack of freedom. He designed title pages for such popular pieces of music as "Kittie Darling" and "Oh, Whistle and I'll Come to You, My Lad."

When he went to Bufford's he was rather undersized, delicately built. He did all his work standing, as he did not want to lean over a desk all day, for fear it would make him round-shouldered. He worked steadily, faithfully, and quietly, he never showed whether he was pleased or angry, for he took praise and criticism with much the same expression.

To make himself look older and more manly when he went to Bufford's he tried to grow a beard! Imagine a nineteen-year-old boy of today with a beard, but it was the time of beards (you recall the pictures of the officers in the Civil War?). His beard came in very scantily and in funny patches, and he said of it solemnly, with that dry humor of his, "My beard is in house lots, isn't it?" While he was at Bufford's he often got up at three to fish before breakfast, and after fishing several hours he returned by bus (not

45

your idea of a bus, but an affair pulled by horses). He was always punctual at the shop.

Once, years after, Winslow met a man who said to him, "How is it I do not remember ever meeting you in Cambridge, yet we must have been there at just the same time?" To which Homer retorted, "I remember you very well, for you were ten years older than I and you used to push me off the steps sometimes, when I was trying to hook a ride on the omnibus to Boston."

Oh, how he hated the drudgery—or "slavery," as he called it, at Bufford's! He never forgot it the rest of his life, for he felt he had held "his nose to the lithographer's stone" long enough. He determined, when he left Bufford's at twenty-one, never in his life to have any other master than himself!

He illustrated for a time in Boston, doing exactly as he pleased, "free-lancing," as the modern artists call it. He once made a ridiculous caricature of a very conceited and well-known Frenchman about Boston, and sold it to his own tailor for a suit of clothes!

When he was about twenty-two he began sending drawings to Harper & Brothers in New York City. *Harper's Weekly* had just been started, and it soon became very well-known for its illustrations. His work was accepted and he sent them many amusing pictures in black and white—scenes of farm life. If you ever look over *Harper's Weekly* of 1859 you will discover that his work is different from the other artists. Already he was his own man, standing on his own feet.

Winslow Homer

Winslow Homer had one steady aim in life; he never wavered, and as he grew older his work grew better and better! He had always known, even as a boy, what he wanted, and he went straight after it. Have you ever heard that line, "The man who seeks one thing in life and but one, may hope to achieve it before life be done"? Well, that was exactly Winslow Homer's idea.

Artists usually enjoy, at some period of their lives, living among their fellow artists and working with them. This is very natural, because they understand and sympathize with one another's work. They learn a great deal, too, from the artists about them. For a time, Philadelphia had been the city to which artists had gone, but in 1859 it was New York City. In and about the celebrated Washington Square were many well-known American artists, living and working together. For many years that section of New York known as Greenwich Village was the headquarters of many artists. Winslow Homer said good-by to Boston in 1859, and went to New York City to seek his fortune. And so, of course, we hear that he went to Washington Square, where many of his artist friends had studios. His studio was in a tower room, and from it he could climb a steep flight of stairs, which was more like a ladder, to the roof. It was this roof which most delighted him, for it was flat and a stone wall was about it, and when he began to paint in oils, he liked to have his models up there to pose for him. It was after he came to New York that he decided to paint and to take it up in earnest. He said he loved the very smell of paint.

When Harper & Brothers heard that he was in New York City, they sent for him and made him an excellent offer to work steadily for them alone. He refused this offer, tempting as it was, for he wanted to be absolutely free, the memory of the "slavery" at Bufford's was still too vivid in his mind, and yet for many years he sent work to *Harper's* as he pleased—in fact, for nearly twenty years! He enjoyed the income he received from his Harper drawings, for it allowed him to be independent.

After he decided to take up painting, he felt he needed more lessons, so for a time he went at night to the National Academy of Design, which was on Thirteenth Street. This Academy, you will be surprised to know, was founded in 1825, and one of the men who helped to found it was Samuel B. Morse, inventor of the telegraph! Samuel Morse himself was an artist, and was the first president of this Academy.

Winslow Homer had some very jolly, happy evenings in that Washington Square studio. There were often a dozen artist friends there at a time, telling stories, singing and working together. And there one might see Winslow Homer in the center of the group, working furiously, under a flickering gaslight, on a drawing that had to be finished at midnight for Harper & Brothers.

"Here, one of you boys," he would shout, joyously, "fill my pipe for me. I am too busy to stop!" Sometimes Winslow Homer would show a playful side of himself to his fellow artists. Once he came into the studio with ribbons of every conceivable width and color sticking out of his pockets. His friends laughed uproariously, but Winslow Homer answered, with that quiet humor of his, that of course he didn't want the ribbons, but every time he saw a pretty face at a ribbon counter he stopped and bought a ribbon for the mere pleasure of speaking to its owner! Although Winslow Homer enjoyed talking to a pretty girl and did not dislike society, he never made any girl a real friend and never cared about one enough to marry her!

In 1861, the course of many lives in America was changed, and of course Winslow Homer's was, with thousands of others! Harper & Brothers sent him as a special artist correspondent at the seat of war. He made some sketches of Lincoln's inauguration. Afterward he was sent to the front, and for some time shared all the excitement and hardships of the soldiers. He was with the Army of the Potomac, and saw much bitter, hard fighting, right in the heart of the enemy's country. He sent back to *Harper's* many vivid sketches, some amusing, some tragic, some pathetic. From them it was easy to see that they were done on the spot, for they were so "real." One of the most famous of these—"Prisoners at the Front"—was at one time exhibited in Paris, and later at Antwerp and Brussels. Throughout the war and for a time afterward Winslow Homer stayed in the South, and sent back thousands of pictures to *Harper's Weekly*.

In 1867 Homer made his first voyage to Europe. A trip to Europe in those days could not be made in five days, and on that long trip over he learned to know the sea and its moods, and deep and strong within him stirred a love and respect for its power, vastness, and majesty! It held him in its spell for the rest of his days. The love born in him on that trip was more important, did more to change his art, than any of the things he saw, people he met in the great artistic city of Paris. He stayed there for ten months, until his funds gave out, and then he returned to America.

What he did *not* do in Paris is more important than what he did do! He did not go to the great art galleries and make copies of famous masterpieces, he did not join with any of the groups of American artists living there, nor did he make friends with any of the French artists. And what he thought of the art and artists he met he never told. Very likely he did not do much, if any, thinking about them. For one thing is very certain—nothing that he saw in France, none of his experiences, had the slightest effect upon his painting, for he came home from Europe to paint in a way more his very own than he had before he went over. Those three thousand miles of ocean, twice crossed, made a greater impression upon him than all the art galleries, artists, and beautiful buildings he had seen!

A lucky chance took him to the beautiful east coast of England, to a quaint little fishing village. He stayed here two years, painting the lovely beach, the high cliffs, the fishermen and their wives; painted shipwrecks and rescues. He came to know intimately the lives of those "who go down to the sea in ships," and he painted them in fair weather and storm. With all his power and honesty he was now painting the ocean and those who live by it and die because of it.

50

While Homer was in England he found a charming little house which pleased him very much, down in this fishing village. It had a tiny garden, and about it was a high stone wall, with one gate, the key of which he kept in his pocket. Here in the garden he could work in peace, without the curious watching over his shoulder (which he hated). As has been said, he could paint from memory, and so he painted vividly, behind his garden wall, the scenes he had just witnessed on the shore.

You have all heard of Jean François Millet, the French painter who painted the peasants of France with so much power and beauty. Undoubtedly, you have seen his "The Angelus" and "The Gleaners." There is something about Millet which very much reminds one of Winslow Homer. It was not what they painted that was alike, except both painted humble, simple, hard-working people, but the way they felt as they worked. Both were men who hated sham and pretensions, and who scorned the "smart people" in society, and who painted the things and people nearest them faithfully and sincerely. Millet painted his peasants in their fields, and Homer painted the fisher folk by their ocean! Both painters were strong, simple men, and men of great independence. Millet was as French as Winslow Homer was American.

When Winslow Homer returned to America after his two years in England, he spent some time painting the seafaring people in and about the beautiful coast town of Gloucester, Massachusetts. His brothers and their families went, one summer, to Scarsboro, Maine, and the whole course and manner of Winslow Homer's life was changed because of his visit to them there. He was completely enchanted by the coast of Maine, and felt that no other spot in the wide world could so satisfy him. Near by, at a place called "Prout's Neck," he built his studio, which was to be his home as well. It was a snug little cottage he built, hardy enough to withstand the fierce "northeasters" that raged along the coast, and in it he lived for nearly thirty years. On the side of the cottage facing the ocean was a fine wide balcony, so that when he was resting he could sit and watch the ocean. Behind his cottage was a lovely garden, fragrant and sweet with old-fashioned English flowers— primroses and cinnamon pinks. About his garden he built a high stone wall, to shut out the curious eyes of prying people. To some, a stone wall means a prison, but to Winslow Homer it meant freedom. Do you remember how he liked his studio on the roof with its wall when he was a young man in New York City, and how he delighted in the garden wall about his little home in England? Behind his stone walls he felt the freest man in all the world because he was master of himself and his little kingdom and his heart was content. He lived alone at Prout's Neck; except for an old man who came in the morning to clean for him, he did all his own work, even his cooking. He lived well, for he liked good things to eat, and he was a first-rate cook, and he had the best of everything sent to him. He had a habit of ordering in huge quantities (which was a good idea, for sudden storms might shut him off from supplies), and when he saw anything he very much

ALL'S WELL *by* Winslow Homer

wanted, he ordered enough for a long stretch of time. This was so even with clothes, for at one time he had one hundred pairs of socks. He said he was afraid they might be "out" of them when he called again! Each year he stayed until December at Prout's Neck, when a ferocious driving snowstorm would nearly bury his little cottage, and then he would fairly dig himself out and go south, to the West Indies, Florida, or the Bahamas, where he would stay until March. While he was south he painted the dazzling, warm, and radiant sky and seas, in water-color, instead of the oils he used in his Northern pictures. Some people think that his brilliant water-colors of Southern seas are as fine as his oil-painting of the cold and stormy coast of Maine. But his whole heart and soul were completely wrapped up in the life along the Northern New England shore, and he is most himself when he is painting its "stern and rock-bound coast."

If anyone has spent a summer on the Maine coast, he may understand how Winslow Homer could so love it. On any summer afternoon one may listen to an old sea captain tell his adventures, and thrill at his bravery in the face of storm and fog (fog is the most treacherous peril the seafaring man knows). And on any summer morning one may lie in bed and in the gray dawn hear the fishermen pass under one's window (even if it is a stormy morning), to their little boats to chase huge horse mackerel (or tunafish, as they are called) or set lobster pots, or "fish for herring fish" that abound in the treacherous sea! One may watch them bring in their nets, or return disappointed and empty-handed. There are fogs that steal in over the land swiftly, there are sudden squalls, and the long days of rain of a "sou'easter." The fisherman's life is filled with excitement, danger, and bitter disappointment. Perhaps, some morning, one may see a ship high and dry on the rocks, where it had been dashed the night before in a storm, with the fishermen sitting forlornly and dismally looking at their "catch," and the entire shore covered with shining silver herring, and just above the sea gulls shrieking and storming, ordering everyone away so they might have their feast! What a cruel disappointment to the poor fishermen, for all their weary toil had been in vain!

All of these things Winslow Homer has put into his paintings, "The Fog Warning," "The Wreck," "The Gale," "Early Morning after a Storm at Sea," "The Banks Fishermen," and "The Coast of Maine." Some think this last one is Winslow Homer's masterpiece, for it gives one the feeling of grandeur, and the height of those majestic cliffs, and the power of the ocean roaring in against them. This painting is in the National Art Gallery at Washington. If you ever see it, be sure to look for the tiny figures of some people standing on the top of the cliffs, and from their size you can realize the tremendous height of these giant cliffs!

In order to see the storms better in all their fury that beat, raged, and roared about Prout's Neck, and to feel a part of them, Winslow Homer built a portable studio, set on runners. This he moved about out-of-doors, as he wished. It was a tiny studio only six feet by eight feet, with one door and a big plate-glass window. During a wild "nor'-easter" he would take this little studio out, and paint as the storm beat against its sides. No wonder he could paint the masterpieces of the sea that he did, and make us forget, in looking at them, "the paint," and feel, instead, the spray and smell the salt and hear the mighty roar of the surf. He made himself an actual part of it all; that is why his paintings of the sea are so very real. He sat with his face against the oncoming storm and wind, and they seemed to go straight through his body and come out of his fingers, right on to the canvas he was painting.

When he came to paint "All's Well" he made very sure that every detail would be true and honest. He planned to paint a night watchman on a boat, calling out his "All's Well" in the dead of the night. So, in the first place, since it was to be in the night, he decided to paint at night. Of course, in order for him to see it had to be a moonlight night, and as all nights are not made bright by the moon, he could not touch it for days at a time. When the moon was full and high in the heavens, he set up his easel, had an old fisherman dressed in oilskins pose for him, and so painted the scene as he saw and felt it. Behind the night watchman he wanted to have a ship's bell show, and he searched high and low in all the junk shops for a bell to suit him, but he could not find anything that satisfied him. So he modeled out of clay a bell that pleased him, and set it up behind the sailor he was using for a model. He went aboard many ships in the harbor of Boston so that he might be sure his rigging was just right. The picture is simple—

so much is left out; we have only the strong fine head of the old night watchman, one hand upraised, the bell, a few ropes, the edge of the boat, and a silver thread of ocean beyond. But this is enough; the picture is beautifully planned, beautifully spaced. The hand is where it should be; everything is given its right amount of space, so that his story is told as simply as possible. You have written a story in school and called it a composition, and an artist also calls the story he decides to tell in his picture a "composition." How little there is in the picture, and how much it makes us feel! We do not need the entire ship, or the full-length portrait of the man, for as it is we can feel enough! We feel the hour is late and all below are deep in sleep, and that there will be no sound to answer the watchman's cheering message; nothing will break the vast stillness but the swishing of the waves against the sides of the boat. The wind will carry his voice far across the boundless stretch of ocean and the boat will sail on this night upon its peaceful way.

Although Winslow Homer lived almost like a hermit at Prout's Neck for years, and preferred to talk with coast guardsmen, fisherfolk and his simple, uneducated neighbors, and was not very cordial to strangers who wanted to look in at him, there are many sweet and generous stories told about his gentle kindness. Every summer his brothers and their families (to whom he was devoted) came to Scarsboro, along with many other summer visitors. They knew him to be as tender as a woman if anyone were sick or in trouble. His sister-in-law was ill all one long summer, and every morning Homer would present himself at her door with a quaint nosegay of old-fashioned flowers gathered from his garden. And so it was with anyone who was sick, or if any guests were at his house he presented them each morning with a bouquet. Although he was a blunt man and not much of a talker, he never said harsh or unkind things, and if by chance he said anything that might hurt, he straightway repented and was sorry. Many are the kind things he did "under cover," and so very quietly for he did not like being made a fuss over at all!

Once a man came all the way from New York out of pure curiosity to see the celebrated painter. After he wandered about Prout's Neck for a while, he met a poorly dressed man with a fishing-pole, and he stopped him, saying, "I say, my man, if you can tell me where I can find Winslow Homer, I have a quarter for you." The man answered, quietly, "Well, where's your quarter?" After it was given to him, he drawled out, slowly, "I am Winslow Homer."

One of Winslow Homer's paintings, "Eight Bells" (which means "noon"), was sold for $4,700 three years after it was painted, and twenty-three years later it was sold for $50,000. This was in 1922, or twelve years after Homer's death. So, you see, his fame and name are now of greater worth than they were at the time of his death!

In 1910 Winslow Homer was seventy-four and his health began to fail, but he would not give up, would not leave his beloved Prout's Neck, even though his devoted brothers asked him to. He was like the stern, courageous old sea captain he loved so well; he would face the on-coming storm and would not give up his ship. He did not like to have people ask him about his health; he refused to complain about it. One of his best friends, a Mr. William Howe Downs, wanted to write a book of his life; but Homer at first refused; he said such a book, if published, would "kill him," for he couldn't see why people would be interested. But as he knew Mr. Downs to be a faithful friend, at last he consented. He never lived to see it published. In his studio he worked until the last, for he left us one unfinished painting, which you may see if you ever go to the Metropolitan Museum in New York City.

His brothers, who loved him devotedly, were with him when he heard his last call. As the vikings of old stayed upon their ships and put out to sea when they were dying, Winslow Homer stayed in his studio by the ocean. Just beyond, the Atlantic rolled out its deep and solemn music, like the great chords on a mighty organ. He died as he wished, facing the sea he loved so well.

No artist was more intensely American than Winslow Homer, for he was as much a part of America as the rugged, majestic shores of New England, and no artist has brought us a finer promise that America must have an art that is all her own!

IV

JOHN QUINCY ADAMS WARD

America's First Great Sculptor

RT IS LONG," LONGFELLOW SAID IN HIS POEM, "A PSALM OF LIFE," BUT HE DIDN'T SAY JUST HOW LONG! IT *IS* LONG, VERY, VERY LONG, FOR SCIENTISTS TELL US now it is probably a half million or a million years long! They are not sure whether the traces of ancient artists in southern Africa are five hundred thousand years old, or a million years! What difference does a half million years or so make to us, for it is as easy, or as hard, to imagine a million years as a half million!

What kind of people were those who lived thousands and thousands of years before the dawn of history? How did they spend their days? If they had among them singers, dancers, poets, judges, prophets, or mighty kings and chieftains, we have no way of knowing. The songs they may have sung have been swept away into boundless space by the winds of countless years, the words of their wise men are forever lost, the glory of their leaders vanished. How do we know they lived? What do we know of them? It is through the work of their artists, for it is only that which has stood the wear and tear of time! They were not clumsy, crude artists, these prehistoric men, for every blow of their tools upon stone tells us of their skill, originality, and imagination.

The artists whose stories we have been reading did not work on stone, but on canvas with paint and brushes. An artist who works on stone, marble, or bronze is as much an artist as the painter, and his work has been able to last through the centuries far better, for the material with which he is working does not perish in the course of ages. The first great painters were the Italians; their first master painter was Giotto, who was born twelve hundred years *after* Christ. The Sphinx and pyramids of Egypt were built nearly three thousand years *before* Christ! Before the Egyptians we had these prehistoric artists of a half million or a million years ago! Now we have some idea of how *long* art is!

Artists whose work is in stone, marble, or bronze are called architects and sculptors. Throughout the ages they have most often worked together. The architect plans and designs a building; in the past it may have been an Egyptian tomb, a Greek temple, a Roman amphitheater, or a Gothic cathedral of Christian times. It was the sculptor who made the statues that were to adorn the finished building and be a part of its beauty. Of course, not always the sculptor made statues for a building; sometimes he made a statue as a monument, to honor a god, or some great person, alive or dead, which stood on a public square.

This story is to be of a sculptor, America's first great sculptor—John Quincy Adams Ward. He is to sculpture in America what Gilbert Stuart was to painting, the first whose work was to stand the test of time. He is often called the "dean of American sculptors." Although, as we have noticed, sculpture is a much older art than painting, it was painting that came first in America. And thereby hangs a tale—a very interesting tale! John Quincy Adams Ward, America's first great sculptor, was born two years after her first great painter had died—in 1830. Up to that time there had been only a very few men in America who dared to be sculptors, for it took a brave spirit to face all the obstacles in the path of a would-be sculptor. There were a few pioneers—Fraser, Greenough, Hiram Powers, and H. K. Brown. Their work was not very original, and to most of us today it is not well known.

But here is the tale of why such an ancient art as sculpture was so slow in showing itself in America. If the early Puritans had little use for painting, they utterly condemned sculpture! Statues to them were out and out wicked and pagan—of the devil himself! They had never seen a cast or a photograph (it was before the camera had been invented) of the beautiful statues of the Greek sculptor, Phidias, or those of the mighty Italian artist, Michelangelo. They had only heard of them, and what they had heard horrified them. Pagan gods and goddesses—men and women not properly clothed! The lovely statue of Venus which is familiar to every school boy and girl in America today would have outraged and scandalized them. Venus, to their way of thinking, should have been modestly dressed in a half dozen petticoats and a long enveloping

61

homespun dress, like their own Puritan maidens. In their homes and in their churches they demanded austere, stern simplicity—no statues in evidence anywhere, above all, not those of false and pagan gods! The only people about them who chose to decorate themselves and their belongings were the savage Indians. The early American settlers did not realize, as we do now, that the American Indian had a beautiful art of his own! They thought their attempts to decorate themselves and their pottery were merely savage, ungodly, and sinful.

Six days of the week these early settlers toiled from sunup to sundown, grubbing, building, fighting Indians and the weather, weaving, baking, brewing, and on the seventh day they humbly bowed their heads in their bare little churches, and thanked their God for what He had in His mercy given them. They had no time during the week to read, and on the Sabbath it must be the Bible; they had no time or desire to read of the grandeur and the glory of the art of the ages. It was not for them!

This attitude of the early Puritan toward sculpture lasted for a long, long time. Sons thought as their fathers had, and they in turn told their sons. And so, the first few men who longed to be sculptors took themselves out of America just as fast as they possibly could and went to Italy. They could not study here!

A sculptor must know the proportions of the body— its anatomy—and he can't study the form of a body through clothes. Imagine a doctor studying anatomy through hoopskirts, capes, and what not! Art schools were not permitted to have "life classes" until after the Civil War. Up to then they were positively forbidden. Today all art schools have their "life classes," and students, without question, draw or model right from the human body. This is, of course, as it should be.

Besides all these obstacles in their way, the first sculptors had another, which was very discouraging and exasperating. There was no good marble in America with which to make statues, nor were there the proper sand and plaster to make bronze. A sculptor had to send all the way to Europe for his materials, and in the weeks and weeks of waiting for it to arrive by way of a slow-moving sailing-vessel, he could easily lose heart in the whole undertaking. If the order went wrong or was not just right, it meant months of idly waiting for it to be made right—if it ever was! No wonder our first sculptors "took themselves to Europe as fast as they could"—to Italy or France. Their work was not very good, for they merely imitated! "Beware of imitations" is a popular modern slogan, and it certainly applies to art! They made statues of "dying gladiators" or Greek slaves, after the fashion of the ancient Greeks, or they copied the sculptors working in Italy at that time (and they were not the best that Italy had). Then a very wonderful thing came to pass for art in America after the Civil War! Something that was to make artists in America more independent, make them feel they need not copy and imitate.

Every boy and girl in America knows one date—1776! Every boy and girl has celebrated that fourth day of July

63

since he or she was old enough to celebrate anything—
our Declaration of Independence! We had determined to
be a free, separate, and independent country. Independence
Day is our greatest holiday. One hundred years after that
famous date, in 1876, the newest nation—the baby
among the nations—decided to celebrate its "first birthday." What is a hundred years when you think of the
ages of the other countries? Only two hundred years before
it had been a vast wilderness filled with savages, and for
only one hundred years a nation among the nations of the
world! It was decided to celebrate this remarkable birthday with a World's Fair at Philadelphia. The whole world
was invited to come and see just what this very young
nation had done in one short century!

You have, very likely, seen people getting ready for an
exhibition—perhaps a school exhibition? Everyone is all
keyed up and on tiptoes to do his or her very best. There
is a hustle and bustle, everyone working harder than he
or she ever worked before—eager to give the very finest
display that was possible. Hours and hours of extra toil,
hours and hours of extra planning. That is why exhibitions
are very useful and good once in a while—they spur people
on to working as they never had, inspire them to do their
supreme best. The World's Fair at Philadelphia was like
a big exhibition—it was to show all that had been done
in America that first one hundred years.

The artists, of course, did not want to make a poor
showing—did not want to be laughed at by other countries, or have it said that they were only poor imitators.

64

They were inspired to do their very best. The year 1776 marked our independence as a country, a nation, and 1876 marked a new independence, although no declaration was signed and no new liberty bell rang out the tidings. American artists were determined to work for an art of their own; they believed passionately in an art here in this new country, that was to be strong and original, like the nation itself. Of course, it couldn't come all in a minute, or even a few years, but they believed it would come. America had made an inspiring beginning in that one hundred years; it makes us thrill with pride to think of it. The year 1876 was an important date in the story of art in America!

Among the artists whose work was exhibited at the World's Fair was a young sculptor—John Quincy Adams Ward. How very patriotic and American was the name given to him by his parents, even if it was a mouthful— "John Quincy Adams"—a famous name in the early history of America's independence and in her beginning as a nation. He lived up to the name that was given to him by his devoted and hopeful parents, for his life was independent and courageous. John Quincy Adams Ward with his whole heart believed in the future of American art—in its right to be "free and independent." He believed firmly that American sculptors need not go abroad to study, and that they might be great right here in America. In fact, he pleaded with American sculptors living abroad to come home, for "We shall never have good work at home as long as her sculptors continue to live abroad."

At the time of the World's Fair Ward was forty-six years old, and to you this may not seem "young"! But when we realize that he still had thirty-four years of splendid work ahead of him, we must admit he was far from old. It was due to him, more than to any other sculptor, that the display of sculpture at the World's Fair was a success and that it promised so great a future for American artists.

John Quincy Adams Ward came by his independent, courageous spirit naturally. He had the blood of dauntless pioneers in his veins. He longed, as they had, to blaze new trails for others to follow. Years before, an ancestor had left England to go to the very little town of Jamestown, Virginia. Jamestown had been settled only twenty-five years when the first member of the family arrived—John Ward from Norfolk, England. Of course, like most Virginians, he became a planter and spent his days overseeing the growing of tobacco or cotton. After a few generations, the life of a Virginian planter seemed too safe, too calm and peaceful, for the adventuresome spirit of the "Wards." They did not relish living their lives to the exact pattern of their neighbors. They now had more neighbors, for Jamestown was growing. A Colonel James Ward moved on toward the Virginian border, and was killed fighting Indians. This tragedy did not frighten his son into staying safely back upon the plantation. He felt, since his father had lost his life in the wilderness, that it would seem almost cowardly to think too greatly of his own peace and security. Our country owes its growth to just such dauntless spirits as these. In the face of death they did not turn back afraid, but forced their way on and on into the heart of the vast wilderness. So we read that this son of the Colonel James Ward who was killed by Indians on the Virginian border took his courageous family and traveled over the Blue Ridge Mountains, making their own roads, traveling up hill and down dale through the forests, always with the memory of Colonel Ward's death in the backs of their heads. They plunged on until they had crossed the mountains into Kentucky. He, of course, became owner of large tracts of land, some of which spread into what is now called Ohio. This was William Ward, and he laid out and founded a town called Urbana. He was himself a sturdy pioneer, and so, but in a different way, was his grandson, John Quincy Adams Ward. America's pioneer sculptor was born in the little frontier town laid out by his grandfather in 1830.

John Quincy Adams Ward as a boy was no different from other boys about him; he liked the things that they liked and did the things that they did. He was ready for all the sports and games there were to be had. In his games and sports he never faltered; he was the type of boy who leads, not follows. He was brought up on a farm, and his days were spent like those of all other boys on a farm. He attended the little country school, and in this he began his education, as so many great Americans have.

In an idle moment one day, when he was a half-grown

67

boy, he picked up some clay from his father's farm and
began modeling it in his fingers. The feel of it fascinated
him, and he suddenly became absorbed and interested in
what he was doing. It was excellent clay for modeling—
potter's clay—the kind from which pottery is made. Pok-
ing it here and there, shaping it this way and that, became
more and more interesting to him. Near him stood a
curious, open-mouthed little group of companions, and,
fired by their interest, he began working in earnest. Before
their wondering eyes began to appear the head of an old
negro slave who lived in the neighborhood. Probably none
were more surprised than the young artist himself. It had
all seemed like an accident, a strange adventure—his dis-
covery of the fine modeling clay, and most of all his unexpected skill in handling it. His family were surprised and
delighted. To them it seemed nothing short of marvelous!
And it *is* to be marveled at that this boy brought up on
a farm, with no knowledge of art or of sculpture, should
suddenly find himself able to model an excellent likeness
of an old neighbor. Of course, from then on, clay lured
him, attracted him, and in all his spare moments he worked
with it. In his secret heart he came now to cherish an
ambition; he was afraid to tell anyone, above all his companions who worked on farms. He felt that they would
surely laugh or stare at him as though he had gone plumb
crazy! Imagine telling a few Tom Sawyers and Huckle-
berry Finns that you wanted to study and work very hard
to be an artist and to make a living from sculpture! They
surely would have "ha-ha-ed." They admired his work; it

was a good trick, and plenty of entertainment, but as a living! No, John Quincy Adams Ward knew better than to share his secret ambition with anyone, especially at this time, when one American sculptor was creating all kinds of excitement and scandal.

Powers was this daring sculptor's name—Hiram Powers. He had made a statue called "A Greek Slave" (this was when American sculptors were more or less imitating). It was a beautiful statue and to us it seems very strange that there should have been all this commotion and uproar over it simply because, like many Greek statues, or those fashioned after them, it was nude. A committee of clergymen was appointed to view the statue and decide whether or not it might be exhibited to the public. Fortunately, the committee had the good sense and an appreciation of what was beautiful, for they gave their approval. After the stupid objection was removed, the statue was shown in many cities. At last it came to a city near the home of young Ward. He had heard all the sensation about it, but he wanted to see it, not out of curiosity, but because he had heard it was beautiful. He was still cherishing his very dear and secret ambition, and he longed to see the work of a real sculptor. The lovely marble statue decided him; he was determined that the things he had been modeling in clay should some day be chiseled from this beautiful gleaming white marble! Then and there he made a resolution that he was going to be a sculptor, no matter what toil it cost or what obstacles lay in his path. His only disappointment that day was the fact the sculptor of this lovely marble was nowhere about. He longed to shake his hand and to thank him for the pleasure that his work had given.

His family, like so many families, had other ideas for their son's future. He was to be a doctor, even though he did not show the slightest liking for the profession. Sometimes good fortune comes from what at first seems to be bad fortune, for his health failed and he had to go away for a long rest. Had his health not failed, perhaps his family would have insisted upon his being a doctor. And maybe, in the end, he would have given in, because, after all, there was very little on the farm or in the small town about it to help or encourage him to be a sculptor. It was decided that he be sent to visit his sister in Brooklyn, New York, for a change of scene and rest. This visit made because of ill health was to bring him the very best of good luck.

One day as he was walking near his sister's house, he passed the open door of a sculptor's studio. Half shyly, he stood and watched the scene within; it fascinated him and held him spellbound. He was reluctant to leave the doorway, sorry to turn his back upon something which so strongly appealed to him. On his daily walks from then on he always managed to pass that door, in fact he fairly haunted the spot. Finally he managed to get up courage enough to go into the studio. It belonged to Henry Kirke Brown, one of the earliest of American sculptors. The secret ambition which young Ward had been so long cherishing could no longer be kept a secret; he was bursting with it, he must tell some one. The some one was his sister, for on returning from a visit to a real studio he could keep it in no longer. His sister was eager to help him; she even went to Brown and asked him if he would take her brother for a pupil. Brown was not very sure he wanted him; probably he thought a country boy without any training would be hopeless. The boy's earnestness, his eagerness, however, encouraged the sculptor somewhat, so he at last agreed to take him as a pupil. Then Ward had to get the consent of his family to let him live in New York, give up the farm, give up all hopes of being a doctor. It was something of a struggle, because no one knew whether he had any great talent (even in his own heart he was not sure). In the end everyone gave up fighting against the boy's ambition, and he came to New York— for one year! That one year stretched on and on until it became seven. He was a boy of nineteen when he first began his lessons; he was over twenty-six when he decided to strike out for himself. Brown, after a very short time, was so impressed by the boy's intense interest and skill, that he made him his assistant. There was plenty for the young assistant to do in the sculptor's studio even from the first. The clay had to be kept moist, then it had to be kneaded until it was smooth and the proper consistency for modeling. While he was helping his master he was learning drawing and modeling; later he learned to carve marble and work with bronze. Most modern sculptors model their figures in clay first, and let their assistant copy it in marble. The modeled clay figure or group is like a design or plan, from which the finished work is made.

71

Young Ward had a hand in everything, for Brown trusted him with even his best and finest work. When Ward himself became a sculptor, he never allowed any assistant to finish his work, for he did it all from first to last, like the ancient sculptors. For this he was often called "old-fashioned."

However, Brown was very fair and generous with his young assistant, for when he had finished his very best piece of work, the one of which he was most proud, he insisted that the boy take a chisel and mallet and add his name. This was a bronze statue of George Washington on a horse, and it stands in Union Square, New York City. If you look, you will see the name of J. Q. A. Ward, Asst. 1854, under the signature, H. K. Brown, Sculptor.

A bronze statue is not made in one piece, but is cast in numerous pieces which are finally riveted together. Young Ward spent many days *inside* George Washington's horse, pounding at the rivets, pounding hard enough to give the poor horse a fine old stomach ache! But the rivets held and that is what mattered. Ward said afterward he spent as many days inside that horse as Jonah spent inside the whale!

After this piece of work was finished, Ward felt that he was old enough and capable enough to be his own master. His first choice for a statue was not a "dying gladiator" or a Greek statue, but one that was wholly and entirely American—an Indian. Of course, he could have had a model come to his studio, all dressed up as an Indian, but a white man in Indian trappings did not seem real to

INDIAN HUNTER *by* John Quincy Adams Ward

him. To get the true inspiration for his first piece of work he did not look to Greece or Rome, but very deliberately turned his back on them and traveled in the opposite direction into the very heart of the great Northwest. He was striking out in an independent fashion! He lived with the Indians, on their plains, visiting many tribes and making many sketches and models. In this way, right among the Indians he got the true feeling that he wanted. This first statue was called, when finished, "The Indian Hunter."

The Park Commission of New York City accepted it at once, and it was placed in Central Park. There it is, just where it should be, out under the skies, among the trees and bushes. How much more natural for an Indian hunter to be in such a setting than out on a city street or cooped up in a museum.

This statue is of an Indian and his dog out on the trail of their prey. The dog is quivering with excitement, eager to bound ahead, but his cautious master is holding him back. The Indian is bent low, but his body is tense and with a stealthy tread is stealing forward. Although his eyes gleam, he is still and silent. In another second he shall have brought down his victim at his feet; then he may let out a whoop of triumph. As we look at the statue we are tempted to glance over our shoulders to see what the Indian is gazing at so intently, as though we expected to see a stag a few feet away! This bronze Indian and his dog makes us think of days long vanished, when perhaps at this very spot a real Indian prowled among the trees and bushes! Such a statue seems just the happiest and best

73

choice for America's pioneer sculptor, for it is so thoroughly and entirely American.

For fifty years Ward worked in and about New York City. From that first piece of sculpture, "The Indian Hunter," to his last, his work was dignified and distinguished. Not only was it dignified and distinguished, but it was thoroughly American. He was happiest always when he was doing something that was inspired by his country's history, for he seldom chose a subject that was foreign. Among the four of his statues which are in Central Park only one was not American, and that was his Shakespeare. This was not his own choice, for he had been asked to do it; it was a commission.

In reading over the long list of his work we find that he had made a statue of each period of our history. First, the Indian; then "The Pilgrim"; then heroes of the Revolution—Washington, Israel Putnam, and Lafayette. His statue of Henry Ward Beecher recalls the struggle to free the Negro, for Beecher was an ardent preacher against slavery; then we have his Horace Greeley and his Garfield. To this list of heroes and patriots we must add the name of Admiral Dewey, for Ward designed a group which decorated the Victory Arch under which one bright triumphant day the conquering hero, Dewey, rode! Although this arch was to last for but one brief day, it was one of the finest things he had ever done.

John Quincy Adams Ward had always, with great simplicity and courage, practiced what he preached in his long years of splendid work—that American sculptors could find their inspiration right here on American soil. He had made one trip to Rome, and although he was deeply impressed by the splendor of her art, he came back to his native soil determined not to follow in the footsteps of other masters. He felt strongly that America could and should have an art that was all her own. His work certainly shows us that he was faithful and devoted to his ideal.

Fifty years, we have learned, is a very, very short time in the history of art. But in Ward's fifty years many changes had come to art in America, for sculptors, painters, and architects had been making great strides. In 1876, at the Centennial in Philadelphia, the sculptors of America had indeed made a declaration of independence, led by Ward. A declaration that was not put down in writing or proclaimed by a Liberty Bell! Their signatures were not on paper, but chiseled into the stone of their statues. Each piece of sculpture and each sculptor's name declared that we as a country must have an art that was free and independent. It was not a very big display, nor, perhaps, a very great one at the time, but it was fine enough to inspire other artists to struggle and work for an art that was to be America's own and a part of the glorious history of art throughout the long ages.

V

JAMES McNEILL WHISTLER

America's Master Painter

ALMOST EVERY BOY AND GIRL HAS AT SOME TIME OR OTHER MADE OR DONE SOMETHING OF WHICH THEY WERE PROUD, SOMETHING THEY HAD TAKEN GREAT PLEAS-ure in doing. Perhaps it was a drawing, the singing of a song, a "piece" played on a violin or piano, or something that was cooked, sewed, or made in the workshop. Oh, we all have, whether we are young or old, and a few words of praise do fill us with a secret delight! But instead of these few words of praise, had some one actually laughed and asked, "Well, what in the world is it? What is it all about?" you can imagine how disappointed you would have felt! Some children, even if they are hurt (and who isn't?) by ridicule of any kind, do not run away, but make believe very hard indeed that they don't care, "show off" a bit and answer up with excuses. It is braver to stay, isn't it, and put on a "good face"? If this has ever happened to you, or if you could imagine how it would have felt, you will understand better, and have more sympathy for the supremely great artist, James McNeill Whistler. He loved his work far more than most of us do, and was more

76

serious about it, and yet at one time people joked about it, laughed at it. He knew what it was to have them say, "Well, what on earth is it all about?" He did not run away, but stayed and faced them all with great courage. Yes, and he retorted, laughing at them, taunting them a little, saying sharp funny things that were written up in newspapers, which amused everyone—but those whom he was making fun of! Of course, it must have hurt him, and disappointed him, and even angered him to have the beautiful work he loved so, mocked and not understood. His paintings were very original—very different from the works of most artists—and that is why, at first, he was not understood. In many ways he is the greatest American artist and one of the world's great masters. His quick, sharp, sometimes insolent retorts to those (most often ignorant) who laughed at him make interesting reading, and we will find that his story is an unusual one.

James Abbott McNeill Whistler was born July 10, 1834, at Lowell, Massachusetts. That is what the records show; but Whistler always took the keenest delight in switching his birthplace about (as though one could choose where one was born!). Sometimes he said he was born in Baltimore, Maryland, sometimes in St. Petersburg, Russia, and once, when a young girl asked him where he was born, he answered, solemnly:

"My child, I wasn't born; I came from above."

In this sort of nonsense he took an unholy delight. Perhaps he thought it was all people deserved who asked personal questions, but most likely he answered so because

77

it amused him and those about him. One day, when he was a man nearly seventy, a stranger approached him in the Ritz-Carlton Hotel in London and said:

"You know, Mr. Whistler, you and I were born at Lowell, Massachusetts, and at very much the same time. There is only a difference of a year; you are sixty-seven and I am sixty-eight." Very likely Whistler thought the man was being too familiar, but he answered, with all politeness: "Very charming! And so you are sixty-eight and born in Lowell, Massachusetts. Most interesting, no doubt, and as you please. But I shall be born when and where I please, and I do not choose to be born at Lowell, and I refuse to be sixty-seven!"

Whistler repeated this story and was much amused over it. To him it was an entertaining way of letting the man know he didn't like his prying into his affairs, even if it were only on the subject of his birthplace.

There is a record of James Abbott McNeill Whistler's being christened in St. Anne's Church, Lowell, Massachusetts, November 9, 1834. What a mouthful of a name, and Whistler himself had some difficulty deciding what to do with his names and initials. At one time he decided to drop the "McNeill," but he discovered that the initials of the name that was left spelled J. A. W., which did not please him at all. He was always ready to talk, and he was afraid some "smart Aleck" would take advantage of that word "jaw" and tell him it was most appropriate. Neither did he like the initials of his name as it was, because then

78

it was J. A. M. Whistler. He finally used the "N" instead of "M" in McNeill, and dropped the name "Abbott."

The men of Whistler's family, including his father, Major George Washington Whistler, were many of them army officers, graduates of West Point, and a goodly number were parsons. The first Whistler in America had come from the Irish branch of the Whistler family. They arrived in America in 1777. In many respects James (or Jimmie, Jemmie, Jammie, Jim, as he was called in boyhood) took after his father, for his father had always been somewhat wild, and very original, and had always stood A-1 in drawing at West Point. Major Whistler also had been fond of music in his cadet days, for he played a flute which won for him the nickname "Pipes."

Major Whistler stood for all that is best and fine in the West Point traditions—a gentleman, brave and honorable—and Whistler's mother is described as "one of the saints of the earth." She was very gentle and a devoted mother, but as strict as a Puritan.

Oh, what an event was Saturday afternoon in the Whistler family when "Jimmie" was a boy! There was much hustling and hurrying about—clothes had to be put in spic-and-span order, heads scrubbed, shoes shined, pockets emptied of whistles, tops, marbles, and all the rest of the startling assortment of things that find their way to a boy's pockets—for everything in the house and everybody in the house had to be put in perfect order for the next day. No toys, no playthings of any kind, were in sight on the Sabbath. The only reading in the entire household was the reading of the Bible. They kept the Sabbath in the strict way of the early Puritans.

Jimmie was a beautiful baby, although never strong or big, for he suffered from rheumatic fever, which weakened his heart. His mother always said that he was very brave and sweet in his illness. He was an unusual child—a little wild and excitable, but with an exceptionally good-natured disposition. One day when he was only four an aunt came into a room looking for the baby boy, to whom she was devoted. When she called him there was only a muffled sound, and a faint answer came from under the dressing-table. She leaned over and pulled him out from under it, by one arm and one leg. He had been lying on his stomach, drawing, in peace and quiet. The family were very proud of that drawing, and it was very strong and remarkably firm for a child of four.

When Jimmie was eight the Tsar of Russia, Nicholas I (for that was seventy years before the Russian revolution, and Russia had "Tsars"), sent a commission around Europe and America to find the best method, and the best man, to supervise the building of a railroad from St. Petersburg to Moscow. Major George Whistler was an engineer at West Point, and the commission decided that he was the best man for the undertaking. It was a great honor and the salary was very large. Major Whistler resigned his position in the United States army, and went to Russia. He left his family behind him for a while, but a year later sent for them to come to him.

It was a very long, hard, and unhappy trip for Mrs.

Whistler and her three boys, the youngest only a baby. Much of the journey from Germany to Russia had to be made in carriages, as there were no railroads. The baby died on the way.

St. Petersburg in those days was very different from the city it is today, and, as you know, even its name is not the same, for it is now called Leningrad. Powerful nobles lived in splendor in great mansions, about which were wide parks with their sparkling fountains and lovely gardens. The mansions had vast rooms filled with beautiful paintings and treasures which were priceless. The nobles were very wealthy, the peasants very poor, in those days. Major Whistler and his family, of course, were known to the most powerful in the land, for the Tsar made a favorite of him.

It was certainly a change from a New England city! However, Mrs. Whistler, like her husband, was an ardent and devoted American. When she reached Russia she decided that she would not live in hotels, but that she would make an American home, if she possibly could, for herself and family right in the very heart of the Russian capital. She saw to it that her children had American food and that they celebrated American holidays, even to a turkey at Thanksgiving, and fireworks on the Fourth of July! Many of their friends were American. Their Americanism was as much a part of them as their religion.

Their days in Russia were very interesting, thrilling, and certainly never to be forgotten. Mrs. Whistler tried to keep her boys well behaved, but her strictness did not mean that she would not allow them to stay up at night to see gorgeous fireworks, and oh, what marvelous times they had skating and coasting! Jimmie loved his dancing-lessons and would not have missed them for the world! Those were days of enchantment, sounding more like the days in a fairy tale than real experiences.

One day Jimmie and his mother had been driving through the grounds of a grand duke, and he had seen some of its beautiful works of art. His mother asked him if he would like to be a grand duke when he grew up, and own all these lovely things, even to a room filled with paintings? "No, indeed!" Jimmie answered. "There wouldn't be any freedom at all, with a footman always at one's heels!"

All good Russians, of course, learn other languages, for Russian is too hard a language for the rest of Europe, and they learn French almost as quickly as their native tongue. The Whistler children had to practice reading English every afternoon to their mother, so that they would not forget it, for they spoke most of the time in Russian and French. Of all his school lessons, none fascinated him more than drawing.

One day Jimmie stood with some nobles watching a brilliant military parade, his eyes sparkling with excitement. The men were amused at his ardor and asked him if he were going to wear a uniform when he grew up.

"Oh yes, indeed!" he answered.

"A Russian uniform?" he was asked.

"No, no!"

"English?"

"No, indeed!"

"American?"

"Of course," he answered.

Jimmie was gay and bright and fearless and considerate of others, but most of all of his mother. He was beautifully devoted to her all his life. Even as a child some people did not understand him, because he was unusual, and they just stared at him in surprise, but those who did understand him were fond of him and were delighted by his sweetness and charm.

The Emperor or Tsar, had intended inspecting the new railroad when it was finished, but had postponed doing so. At last he made a big occasion of it, and invited the whole Court to go with him and see it. The day after the inspection, the Tsar held a wonderful reception to the Court in honor of the American engineer. He kissed Major Whistler on both cheeks and pinned upon his coat a medal of the Order of St. Anne. He asked Major Whistler if he would like to wear a Russian officer's uniform, but he refused. Many honors came to him, but he had worked too hard, and through one hot summer he continued working, even while the dreaded disease, cholera, raged. At last he caught it, and because his health had been weakened he could not fight it, and so died.

The Emperor was fond of the Whistler boys and did not want them to leave Russia; he suggested that they be educated in the school for Court pages. Mrs. Whistler declined, for this certainly would make her sons more Russian than American. She wanted to get them back to America and educate them, as so many of the men in the family had been, at West Point. The Emperor sent them part way on a barge of state, and they left Russia with a royal farewell.

The Whistler boys, up to the time of their father's death, had been brought up like young princes, but once back in America everything was different. Their mother's income was so very small that they could afford only to rent part of an old farmhouse. They moved to the town of Pomfret, Connecticut, to be near a very excellent school whose principal had once been a West-Pointer, before he had become a parson and a school-teacher. Jimmie's drawings at this school were much spoken of, for he made caricatures and portraits of his friends. With his teachers and with his fellow students he was very popular.

Mrs. Whistler was very proud of her son's talent for drawing, but she could not see it as a future occupation. There was to her only one career for a "Whistler," and that was West Point. She wanted her boy to follow in his father's footsteps. It was not simple to get Jimmie into West Point, because he was so small, but with the personal aid of Daniel Webster, who had thought a good deal of Major Whistler, the boy was entered. At that time Robert E. Lee was the head of West Point.

Oh, the interesting stories that have come to us of those West Point days! Jimmie was always doing and saying something unusual, for if the truth must be told, the "usual" thing at West Point did not appeal to him at all. He was no more suited to West Point than another distinguished American—a young poet, Edgar Allan Poe.

84

West Point does not train poets and artists, and so it is no fault of West Point, or the poets' and artists', that they don't succeed in getting on together! Jimmie *did* get his first real drawing-lessons at West Point, from a teacher named Weir. He stood "A-1" in drawing—and at the foot of the class in almost everything else. In spite of his failures in his subjects, West Point liked Jimmie and Jimmie liked West Point; for all the days of his life he was very proud of his training there, and often boasted of it. But he failed, of course, as a military student, and he had to leave after three years. Although he was discharged from West Point, West Point honors him to this day, for the celebrated sculptor, Saint Gaudens, has made a memorial tablet of him there.

Of course his mother was bitterly disappointed, and in her heart hoped that he would return some day and graduate! His next venture was in the employ of the United States Coast Survey, but he kept this position only a few months, for the maps he had to draw were covered with sketches of people about him. And now what? He certainly had to find something he could do for his future. His mother agreed to let him try out his art—to give him a chance to do what his heart most desired. And so they sailed for Europe, never dreaming, on that voyage, that he would never return to the land of his birth! They went to England first, but Jimmie wanted to go to that famous fascinating section of Paris called the "Latin Quarter," where art students and teachers work and live together. So they went to Paris, his first trip from London to Paris, for he made countless journeys back and forth between those cities during the rest of his life. He began his art-training at a pretty late age—twenty-one! His training in the Latin Quarter and his lessons in drawing at West Point were the only lessons he ever had. They do not seem to have had any good effect on him, for from the first he began to work as no one else about him—or no one else before him! He liked to talk in after years of these days in the Latin Quarter, but he really did not stay there long, nor did it influence him much, if at all.

His first work to receive attention were etchings, not paintings. Paris liked his etchings, but they did not like his first paintings! They were altogether unlike anything they had seen; they could not understand them. He sent some to be exhibited, but they were refused. This probably hurt him, but he showed his "hurt" by being furiously angry instead of quietly taking himself off, ashamed and embarrassed. He left Paris in a temper and went to England.

In Chelsea, England, he and his mother settled down for years in a lovely home which he called "The White House." He and his mother were happy with each other, and they had many distinguished visitors at their home.

People often asked him why he did not go back to America, at which he always said, "When they take the duty off art." The duty on art disgusted Whistler, and he felt America could not love art at all, or it would not make an artist pay heavily for bringing his work here. He said he would hate to have to go over his work, that he was bringing in, with a consul, and pay fees just as an olive or cheese merchant had to do with his wares. However, America did change all this in time, for a Secretary of the Treasury who loved art made a new ruling and the works of American artists, no matter how long the artist had lived abroad, were permitted in free, for which we are grateful! What a tragedy to keep out anything that would add to the beauty of our country!

The very names of Whistler's first paintings confused people, made them laugh and sneer because they could not understand them, for never in the long history of art had an artist chosen such titles for his work—a *musician*, yes, but not a *painter!* He called his paintings "Symphonies," "Nocturnes," "Arrangements," and "Harmonies." When people jeered and laughed at his lovely "Nocturnes," did he run away, hurt and wounded, to hide his face? No, not Whistler! Coolly, deliberately, he dressed himself with insolent care, in a long black coat, high hat, fastidiously arranged his curly black hair so the white streak showed in front, twirled a bamboo cane, placed a monocle in one eye, and faced them all with withering disdain, met their sneers with brilliant sharp retorts of his own! Of course, the newspapers wrote columns upon columns about him. They enjoyed the sensation all this made! They might laugh at him, but they could not ignore him. And sad to say, the American newspapers copied the English ones, and added their ridicule to this native-born American who was bitterly struggling against odds in his search for beauty!

Today all boys and girls in their schools are learning

art, and they have heard their drawing-teacher speak of "color harmony"; in fact, they learn "color harmonies," planning out posters and designs with certain color harmonies in mind. They would not laugh at Whistler's color "harmonies" as the people about him at that time did.

Once in later years Whistler told his art students who came to his studio, to love their brush and palette as a musician does his bow and his violin, for:

"Your palette is your instrument, the colors the notes upon which you play your symphonies." At that time the people were more interested in the "story" of the picture than in the exquisite color or the lovely design it made. For instance, if the picture were of a blacksmith shop, they did not notice the lights and shades in the picture or the fine drawing, but began chattering about blacksmiths they knew, and told stories about anvils and horseshoes! Of course Whistler was interested in the people he was painting, but he was also interested in the color and design he was planning!

In England at this time there was a very popular and celebrated art critic named John Ruskin. An "art critic" is some one who deeply loves art, who studies it and teaches it to the public. Art critics are very necessary, for they help people to understand an artist; but as one artist said, he wanted the critic to be searching for beauty, not looking with a sour face for a case of measles! That meant "critics" should not be looking only for flaws. Ruskin had once been a good and fair critic and he wrote for the London newspapers, and everyone believed everything he said as

MOTHER *by* James McNeill Whistler

gospel truth. Unfortunately, his health (and some say his mind) was failing when he first saw one of Whistler's "Nocturnes" exhibited. A "Nocturne," as perhaps you can guess, is a picture of night, in music; it is a dreamy, soft piece. So Whistler made his "Nocturnes" dreamy, too! The "Nocturne" Ruskin saw first was also called "A Falling Rocket." It was a night scene, showing fireworks, with a falling rocket, very soft and dark in color, with just a few "notes" of bright color. Whistler was asking two hundred guineas for it (a guinea is about five dollars). Ruskin looked at the picture, and then at the price. "What impudence!" he thought; but he did more than think. Unfortunately, he spoke, and worse yet, he published what he thought and what he spoke. And it was published all over England, and here it is: "What impudence! I never expected to hear of a coxcomb ask two hundred guineas for flinging a pot of paint in the public face."

This speech, published broadly over England, could have easily ruined Whistler, and could have driven the "Yankee" (as some called him) out of the country, disheartened and beaten. People hung on Ruskin's words, and to them suddenly Whistler would seem a clown, a faker, a joke! Whistler, as always, did the unexpected, the unusual—he sued Ruskin for libel.

What a trial it was! The public took it as a great show, a lark, and came prepared to laugh and shout and sneer. On the other hand, we have Whistler, with the soul of an artist (easily wounded, even if he did not show it), placing his lovely work he so deeply, tenderly loved, and which he took so seriously, before this mob. A brave man openly to face ridicule, for there is little in this world harder to bear than laughter at something one has loved in honest pride!

They placed his work in court, and then the public began: "Is this thing beautiful?" "Is it a work of art?" "Is it exquisite?" Laughter, laughter and more laughter. No matter how jauntily Whistler twirled his bamboo cane, no matter how much he looked disdainfully through his monocle, or answered insolently, he must have been stung to the heart. The laughter must have smarted and been an agony to him. He did not run away, but bravely and with great courage faced it out. People bet that he would lose, and it did seem he had very little chance of winning. But the judge and jury were ever so much fairer, and more understanding than he might have feared. He won his case, but he was only awarded a farthing—the smallest English coin. To him it meant victory, as much as a five-cent verdict did once to an American President who once sued some one for a slanderous statement. John Ruskin had to pay the expenses of a costly trial, and Jimmie Whistler put his farthing upon his watch chain, and flaunted it the rest of his days!

The trial was disastrous to Ruskin, but it hurt Whistler as well, because people for a while did not come flocking back to be painted. He suffered financially, and money worries piled up; he even had to lose his charming home in Chelsea. Like many artists, he was a bad manager of money. His struggle for real recognition was long and bitter. He was so different that people went on misunderstanding him, criticizing him, and making an enemy of him. He seemed to take this as a part of the struggle, for he wrote a book with the original title, *The Gentle Art of Making Enemies*. Once after an "enemy" had died he said, sorrowfully (although he must have been laughing inside), "I've hardly one warm personal enemy left." Even when he said these things he knew in his heart, and so did the people who loved him, that he would have been happier never to have had an enemy. He craved the regard of everyone, but he would not sit and sulk in silence if he could not have it.

While he was living with his mother in Chelsea he painted one of his most beloved and most celebrated paintings—his "Mother." He loved her deeply, but his love for her was a sacred personal thing between them; he did not want to even call the picture "Mother"; he did not want the wide world to chatter about it and get sentimental about it. So he called it "An Arrangement in Black and Gray." This title, of course, was not understood, nor was it at first appreciated. If you will examine it, you will see how simply it is arranged, or "designed." It was so quiet in color (for the only notes of color were in her sandy hair and the tiny spot of yellow in her wedding ring). It was accepted for an exhibition after heated argument, accepted, but very poorly hung, so it did not show to advantage. He was bitterly disappointed. Today it is considered one of the world's greatest masterpieces, and Americans regret that it is in Paris and not here. A few years ago France hung it in her greatest museum—the Louvre—which contains so many of the priceless art treasures of the world. His painting was the first by an American to hang in the Louvre. It was France who, while he was living, honored him the highest by giving him the distinguished and cherished medal of the Legion of Honor!

Another great portrait of Whistler's is Thomas Carlyle, the celebrated author, who was his personal friend. This, too, is quite simple, like the painting of "Mother." The people of Glasgow collected enough money to pay for it, and it now hangs in the city's art gallery. Another great painting of Whistler's that America has not.

Whistler was passionately fond of children and they in return loved him dearly. One of his greatest paintings, and to some art critics one of the loveliest portraits in the world, was his "Miss Alexander," an exquisite painting of a little girl. It has no equal in modern times except Sargent's portrait called "Beatrice." Alas, too, this painting is not in America, but hangs in London!

Here are some of the children Whistler painted: "Pretty Nellie Brown," "Little Lady Sophie of Soho," "Little Rose of Lyme Regis," "Lilly in Our Alley." These were not the children of the rich, but poor youngsters! He often stopped on the streets to talk with the little waifs and strays, exclaiming, "Oh, the babies, how I love them!" And he painted them as though he loved them. In his last illness he insisted on having the little "Diane," daughter of a friend, near him.

For some time after the trial Whistler lived in Paris with

his wife, a Mrs. Goodwin (the widow of an old friend), whom he married after he was fifty years old. It was in Paris that his work was first truly and kindly recognized. His friends had long called him "Master," and after a big exhibition of his works in Paris, the French accepted the title "the Master," and that was what he was called the rest of his days.

Whistler painted in water-colors almost as well as in oils; his etchings are considered nearly as fine as the great Rembrandt; he is one of the greatest lithographers of all time. A master artist indeed! Although one does not like to mention money in connection with art, it is interesting that one of his portraits (of Lady Meux) a few years ago was sold for $200,000, the highest price ever paid for a modern painting! And to think that John Ruskin thought him impudent to ask for a mere thousand dollars!

How slow were the people about him to recognize his genius, and how bitterly hard was the struggle. He made enemies, it is true (and most great men must), but the tender, sweet, and gentle side of him won loyal and devoted admirers, chief among whom was Joseph Pennell, a great American etcher, who was a personal friend and who has written a beautiful book about him which some day you may read.

His heart was never strong and his health began to fail. He worked feverishly, as though he were afraid he might die before he could finish all the exquisite and lovely things in his soul. Over and over, in these last days, he complained: "I am so tired! I who was never tired."

In his studio he worked harder and harder. Illness made him long to work while it was "still day, for there cometh the night when no man can work." He would forget himself as he painted, standing with his brush in his hand, like a soldier with a sword, ready to fight the last fight, to take the last stand. He could not surrender to anything, even illness, for, after all, there was the blood of soldiers in his veins.

One afternoon he struggled to his feet, his eyes upon his canvas, but the tired body would no longer respond. And so he died, that afternoon in July, 1903. The funeral services were held in the little old church in Chelsea where he often went with his mother, and he was laid beside her in the graveyard at Cheswick.

If in Whistler's life there is much that is sad and bitter, and if we Americans failed and ignored him in life, we are happy that, due to the generosity of an American named Charles Freer, he is now honored in the land of his birth. Charles Freer, an American lover of art and beauty, has given us a rarely exquisite museum—"a temple of beauty," it has been called—in Washington, D. C. And there we may find much of the loveliest of Whistler's work. There is his "Princess from the Land of Porcelain." What an enchanting title! It sounds like the name of a glamorous fairy tale, doesn't it? If his "Mother," "Carlyle," and "Miss Alexander" were here, it would be indeed a shrine to Whistler's art. But here we will find enough of Whistler's work to make us proud and happy that it is where it belongs—in the heart of this nation's capital.

VI

EDWIN AUSTIN ABBEY

A Famous American Mural Painter

THIS STORY IS A TRULY "ONCE UPON A TIME" TALE. IT MIGHT SO WELL BEGIN "ONCE UPON A TIME IN THE QUAINT OLD CITY OF 'BROTHERLY LOVE' THERE was born to a young couple named Abbey a baby boy." This baby boy was destined, one day, to be numbered among the great in the mighty commonwealth of Pennsylvania. Great indeed were the names already written upon her roll of honor—William Penn, Robert Morris, and Benjamin Franklin. As this baby boy grew, his love and devotion for his native state grew with him. Although he was to travel one day, far from his homeland, and was to receive high honors from another country, his last great act of devotion, his supreme task on this earth, was for the glory of his native state, Pennsylvania.

It is hard not to write of Edwin Austin Abbey's life as though it were a glamorous fairy tale—a tale thronged with plumed knights in clanging armor, lovely princesses in flowing robes of rich and shining materials, jolly friars, impish jesters with their saucy tinkling bells, knavish scamps to add their spice and thrill to the story! Oh, it is

95

indeed a "once upon a time" tale! The hero of this story loved the days gone by, the days of pageantry and high romance; they held him in a spell. Not that he was unhappy or discontented in the time in which he lived, for his was always a sunny, bright nature. Had he written instead of drawn, what stories he might have told! Stories that would have made us thrill one minute and chuckle the next! In spite of his love for the days of romance, in spite of the frolicking ways his hands painted in his characters, his last great work for his own state was serious, inspiring, and mighty.

Edwin Austin Abbey was born in Philadelphia in 1852. He was the first son born to his parents. They were to have, later on, another son, and then a daughter. Although his people were never wealthy, they were well bred and very fond of learning. His father, William Maxwell Abbey, was a Philadelphian with English and French blood in his veins. It is claimed that the name "Abbey" had once been spelled "Abbaye" and that it came from a French Hugenot ancestry. His mother's name had been Margery Ann Kipple, the first Kipple coming to America in 1760. Besides this German blood, his mother's family had an Irish strain! English, French, German, and Irish! The good fairies from these lands came from afar to his christening and gave him their best gifts.

Fortunately, no wicked fairy managed to break her way into his American stronghold and upset the promises of his fairy godmothers at the last minute, by putting a curse upon him!

Edwin Austin Abbey

Edwin Abbey's grandmother was one of a host of pretty girls who went to greet the great Washington on his way to New York for his inauguration. She was among the fairest who strewed flowers in his path. So we hear that his grandmother was lovely, and we know that he adored his grandfather, Roswell Abbey. He was proud of his grandmother's beauty, but for his grandfather he had sympathy and understanding. Roswell Abbey was an inventor who spent many hours trying to improve the process of printing. He was not a worldly man, not a business man, but one who daydreamed and had bright visions for the future. Between the inventor and the artist there is this in common—each is seeking to create that which has never been before, and so often they must suffer trying to do it. Edwin's warm heart was touched with pity as he heard of the tricks played upon his unsuspecting grandfather by crafty and dishonest men who often take advantage of an inventor's unworldliness. Roswell Abbey could not leave his family money, but he did leave them something which they felt was wealth—a very fine library. This library was a delight to his grandson, and he felt that his grandfather had left a worthier legacy than gold.

Although, as we have said, the Abbeys never had much money, they had something which was finer—an appreciation for education. They were eager to give their children the best that they could in the way of an education; they always managed to keep them at good schools and give them good books.

Edwin, or Ned, as he was called, had his first photograph taken when he was two years old. The picture shows a very nice-looking, healthy baby boy, but what is really remarkable is that this baby boy had a pencil in his right hand! The story is told that at two he began to draw! What is it that such a baby drew at two? Omnibuses! It seems almost impossible, for the very word "omnibus" seems too tremendous and overwhelming for such a baby. We have shortened that word now to "bus," but even a "bus" seems a large undertaking for one so small. But this is the story we are told—that at two years he sat in his high chair, drawing omnibuses, as an admiring and wondering aunt sat near by, giving him paper and sharpening his pencils. The most remarkable thing about this story is that he even *tried* to draw, and not whether they were omnibuses that anyone would recognize!

Ned had no recollection of this story, but there was one story of his childhood that he never forgot, and told many times when he grew up. He was, evidently like many, far too many, little boys, fussy and cranky about his food. He picked at his food very daintily, enough to worry his mother very much. Getting him to eat as though he enjoyed it wore her out, like it does countless other mothers. One day she was invited to take him with her, visiting. It was with some doubts and fears that she finally accepted, but not without first having a serious talk with her small son. She told him how rude and unmannerly it was to act as though he did not like the food which was given him. He promised obediently to eat cheerfully anything that was offered. His hostess brought him a glass of milk, just as his mother guessed she would, and Ned accepted it with a polite "thank you" and a bright smile. Suddenly he opened his eyes wide with horror, for there in the milk was a big fly splashing about! Ned's expression changed at once, the smile vanished, and he frowned darkly at the fly and its swimming-pool. His mother saw his frown and she quickly gave him a sharp nudge, for she was prepared for a frown. Ned gave her a pleading look, but she shook her head. He must drink that milk; he had promised to take what was given him cheerfully. Manfully he grabbed the glass, and in a few awful gulps had drunk the milk, fly and all! Abbey did not tell this story in after years to little boys who were fussy about their food, as though to say, "If you don't drink a glass of milk and a fly at the same time, you will not grow up to be a famous artist." Oh no! The whole story seemed to him very funny and ridiculous. It was always one of his favorite tales of his childhood—just a foolish story without a moral.

Ned made many drawings when he was very young, and Mrs. Abbey was proud of them, and she did all she could to encourage him. She carefully, tenderly cherished all these earliest drawings. In spite of the story about the omnibuses, and these other early drawings preserved by Mrs. Abbey, Ned always insisted that he never made a drawing worth anything until he was sixteen. But we are sure that, in spite of his insisting upon this, there were many excellent and hopeful drawings before sixteen.

The Abbeys put their two sons into the best classical school in Philadelphia. It was something of a hardship for them to send their sons to such a fine school, but they were very ambitious for their boys. It was their ardent hope that some day they would go to the University of Pennsylvania and follow a profession—the ministry, medicine, or the law. Their fondest hope was that Ned should follow the ministry, although he never showed the slightest interest in it. He once said, in after years, that he must have been a good deal of a disappointment to his parents when he was a boy, for it was his brother who was the excellent scholar, who went to the university, and who followed a profession, not he. His mother cheerfully made the best of her disappointment and encouraged him all she could in his love for drawing. His father, too, managed to overcome his disappointment that his older son would not become a minister.

When Ned was about fourteen he entered the studio of a landscape painter, to take drawing-lessons. This painter was an Isaac Williams, and to the youthful Ned this man of forty-nine seemed more like ninety-four. Ned was not very pleased with his teacher, nor with landscape painting. He grew to detest copying one stupid uninteresting landscape after another. It was not the sort of thing that interested him at all, for he liked drawing people full of life and action. He learned nothing from this teacher, and soon gave up his lessons.

In Ned's boyhood the most popular writer for boys was "Oliver Optic"; it was before the Alger books, of which you may have heard. Oliver Optic ran a magazine called *Our Boys and Girls,* and Ned was a devoted subscriber. Its letter-box interested him very much, and he sent many letters to it, under the name "Yorick." His letters to this column were always very elaborately illustrated with all sorts of interesting and funny sketches. One day he received, to his delight, a letter from a boy who had enjoyed his drawings—a boy who signed himself "Ned Sketchly" —(whose real name was Will H. Low). This boy also liked to draw, and he, too, was an ardent admirer of *Our Boys and Girls*. The two boys had a marvelous time from then on, writing back and forth. "Ned Sketchly" lived in Albany. The boys illustrated their letters, and each one criticized the other's drawings (and none too gently). On one occasion "Ned Sketchly" wrote to Ned Abbey, "Will you, for goodness' sake, send me a decent sketch?" And in return he received a request even more to the point! The correspondence grew so lively that the two boys were eager to meet and curious to see how the other looked. "Ned Sketchly" invited young Abbey to Albany, and it was arranged that he should go. What a flutter of excitement in a home in Albany, and in one in Philadelphia. They wrote an extra number of letters, with elaborate descriptions of how they would know each other when they met in the Albany depot. It would be far too terrible to imagine, if they missed each other! But there was very little danger of this; these descriptions were much too sure for any mistake. The boys fell upon each other's neck with a jubilant shout. "Ned Sketchly's" family were delighted with the charming boy from Philadelphia. During this visit the two young artists formed a sketching club, the members of which almost all grew up to be well-known artists.

Ned's family permitted him later to invite "Ned Sketchly" to Philadelphia. There was no happier boy in all Philadelphia than Ned Abbey the day he sent off that joyous invitation to Albany. "Ned Sketchly" promptly accepted, and it was not long before he was visiting with the Abbeys. The two boys fairly haunted the Pennsylvania Academy of Fine Arts. The bosom friends had a perfect visit, enjoying to their hearts' content the things they both loved so well. In later years they spoke of their youthful friendship with pride and tenderness.

Ned stayed at school until he was sixteen, but as he had never cared much about it, he was eager to leave. His father gave his consent, perhaps with a sigh, for he still hoped the boy might be a minister. With very much the same idea in the back of his head that Winslow Homer's father had had, he put his son in a lithographer's shop. The boy, he hoped, might be apprenticed until he was twenty-one. You remember how Winslow Homer had hated his years of apprenticeship? Fortunately for young Ned, he was to leave long before those five years were up, for he liked this work no better than Winslow Homer had, and he, too, would have grown to feel it slavery.

While he was with this firm he made drawings for all sorts and kinds of school books—spellers, readers, histories, and geographies—and even for Sunday-school books! At sixteen he might rightly have been called an "art editor," because of all the work he had to do.

His pen or pencil moved across a paper as though by magic, almost with the fascinating rapidity of the animated drawings in the movies. One day, while a visitor was discussing business with him, he absent-mindedly picked up a pencil, and as he listened moved his hand swiftly across a paper lying near him. All sorts of queer, funny, and interesting people sprang to life from the tip of his pencil, and moved about—parsons, Negroes, and Chinamen. Then came a troop from out of the Dickens stories—poor little Oliver Twist, the Artful Dodger, Tiny Tim, and the fat Mr. Pickwick! His pencil never faltered. He began with a pair of eyes, giving them just the right expression, and then the rest of the body rapidly followed. One wonders if the visitor was not more fascinated with these drawings than interested in his business conversation.

It was soon recognized that Ned's pencil had a strange magic and that he could make people of other times live and breathe or characters who existed only in books. He delighted all his life in drawing characters from Dickens, Shakespeare, or the *Idylls of the King*. The quaint clothes of other times fascinated him, especially the dress of the seventeenth century. He drew them as though he had intimately known the people who wore them, as though he had been asleep for several hundred years and had awakened with a pencil in his hand, ready to draw the characters with whom he had just been living. More and more at his office he was given orders to draw people of other days.

At seventeen Ned was more than usually attractive. Although he was not very tall, he was a thoroughly fine specimen of a boy. His skin was clear and healthy; his hair, which was neither dark nor light, was thick, and curly about his ears (it was not then considered silly for a boy to have curly hair!). His warm, bright eyes and a flashing smile which showed a perfect set of white teeth gave him an expression which was altogether winning and delightful.

It was at last agreed in Ned's family—as a compromise —that since he was holding a position to please his father, he might take drawing-lessons at the Academy of Fine Arts. These lessons had to be taken, of course, at night. The firm for which he worked was pleased that he was going to go to the Academy, and they gladly gave him a letter of introduction.

On Ned's first visit to the Academy he brought a friend with him. The two boys sat in the hall and waited for some one to come and question them. At last they noticed a man coming slowly, haltingly toward them. Ned watched him intently and decided that it was William Shakespeare come to life, so strong was the resemblance. However, it was not Shakespeare, for Shakespeare's bones were buried in England with his own warning above them that they must not be moved. Not Shakespeare, but a slightly lame professor at the Academy, it was who stood before the two boys, waiting for their letter of introduction.

Ned rose and gave his letter to the professor, who read it slowly. He asked Ned for some samples of his work, and Ned gave him some drawings of Puritans and Indians. The professor stared at them silently for a long time without a word; he was evidently impressed. At last he raised his eyes from the drawings, and after looking at Ned intently for some time, merely said, "Report to the antique class."

Ned did not enjoy the "antique class," for it just meant copying the casts of ancient sculpture. He thought this deadly uninteresting; it was far too lifeless for his taste. Ned grew restless copying one cast for hours on end, as the other pupils seemed to enjoy doing, and he moved about, making a dozen sketches of anything that caught his fancy. Although he did not stay at the Academy for long, it was the only real art training he ever had and he appreciated it all the days of his life.

When he was not at the Academy he spent his evenings at the library, poring over any books which showed the picturesque clothes of other times. He loved to sketch the dress of the people who lived in the days of King Arthur, or in the time of Shakespeare. Often as he drew he longed to go to England and to study these times more closely. Surely in England he could find more material to delight him than in Philadelphia! There were not in that library in 1870 the wonderful amount of material to be found in our libraries today. Some day, he promised himself, he would go to England.

When he was about eighteen he began sending some of his sketches to a magazine—the very same magazine in fact, for which Winslow Homer had worked so many years—*Harper's Weekly*. His first drawings were promptly returned, for, alas! that is the fate too often of first drawings. Finally he had one accepted. It was called "The Puritan." Very likely this was the drawing he had shown at the Academy as a sample of his work. Ten years before, Winslow Homer had started with *Harper's Weekly* as an illustrator.

Edwin Austin Abbey's career had now begun! Harper & Brothers asked him to take a regular position with them. This meant that he must leave Philadelphia and go to New York City to live. His first boarding-house was in Brooklyn. Some cousins occupied the whole second floor; above them lived an amateur artist and his nephew. Ned was overjoyed to have an artist for a companion, especially one who had traveled all over the earth and who had many interesting stories to tell. This artist had gathered a wonderful collection of photographs which were a delight to young Abbey. He pored over them, and in fancy took himself to Italy, Greece, India, and to the foreign art galleries. These three, Ned, the artist and his nephew, had many wonderful evenings together. Ned had a marvelous collection of Negro plantation melodies, which in a soft crooning voice he sang to his banjo. His audience was delighted with his humorous gestures as he sang. There was always a shout of joy at the remarkable somersault he made as he brought his song to a clashing end! Wherever Ned went, he was always the very best of good company and a joy to those about him.

Later on he moved, finding a lodging-house in New York City. Here he was with complete strangers, and although he could be a happy companion, he was at first very shy and sensitive with strangers. In the evenings, in this new boarding-house, instead of frolicking with relatives and friends, he stole away to his own room. There, by candle-light, he drew, working hard on his orders for *Harper's*. Sometimes he needed a model to pose for him, but, not being able to afford one, he stood in front of his mirror, and in the flickering uncertain light drew his own "beautiful figure" (which was his laughing comment on it, later on). He made believe he was all sorts of people, and drew himself in imaginary suits of clothing! Sometimes the room was cold and sometimes he worked nearly all night. He needed the money from his orders, and the orders had to be on time, for a magazine goes to press at a definite hour! At this time he was receiving fifteen dollars a week!

For a while he thought he would try "free-lancing"—that is, not working for any one firm, but taking orders from a number of firms. Besides *Harper's,* he worked for *Scribner's Magazine* and *Saint Nicholas.* But this existence was too uncertain and he decided he would rather work for the Harpers alone, and he went back to them.

Fame was first to come to Edwin Austin Abbey shortly after he moved to the picturesque and celebrated Old University Building in Washington Square. His room on the third floor was the very one in which Winslow Homer had worked and first made his name! It was in this very building, perhaps you remember, that Morse had developed the telegraph? Here, too, Professor Draper had made his experiments with photography and had taken the first picture in America. What a hallowed shrine this building was to Americans of national fame, in art, literature, and invention! What a pity that it was torn down, for it would be so interesting and inspiring to wander about those rooms, hallowed by genius, and read the old signs of men who had passed on but in passing had added to their country's glory!

At the end of Abbey's first year in the Old University Building the newspapers began to shout his praises and loudly proclaim his success. He was jubilant over the notices, and danced and sang with joy as he read them. One day, however, a notice appeared that left him quiet and unhappy. They had compared his work with Homer's and claimed that it was better! "I don't like that, I don't like that!" he said as he paced the floor stormily. He put his coat and hat on and immediately went to call on Homer, who was living near by. It wasn't fair, this comparison! He found Homer somewhat hurt and depressed by the notices, and Abbey's generous attitude soothed him. Abbey brought him back to his room, and together, in a kindly spirit, they talked over their art. Homer at this time had not begun to do the great work which was to make him supreme in his line, for he had not begun to paint the sea. Both men at this time were doing illustrating, and neither man had found yet the work that in the end was to make them great. However, Abbey always painted people and Homer turned his back on them and faced the sea.

Abbey lived well and was a generous host, a generous friend. He was careful of his personal appearance, a charming and delightful guest as well as host. He spent money rather carelessly, for he always wanted the best of materials. His models always had to have the right clothing, no matter what it cost. Dress always fascinated him, especially the dress of other days. Sometimes in those early years he knew

SCENE FROM "JULIUS CÆSAR" *by* Edwin A. Abbey

what it was to be short of funds, as most artists do at some time or other.

Harpers were planning on bringing out a book of verses by the English poet, Robert Herrick, and they wanted it elaborately illustrated. Of course, it was Abbey who was given the commission, for no other illustrator knew English styles and manners as he did. Abbey felt that to get the right feeling and the right material he should go to England. It had long been his wish, and this was his opportunity.

New York City in the 'seventies was gay and interesting, and there was much "wining and dining." Abbey belonged to the Tile Club, a group of very well-known artists. Homer, William M. Chase (the celebrated painter of still life who has many paintings in the Metropolitan Museum), and F. Hopkinson Smith. When the Tile Club heard of Abbey's departure for England, they gave him a wonderful dinner as a send-off. The staff of Harpers' had a breakfast for him at the finest restaurant in the city—Delmonico's. The forty guests were brought to this famous old restaurant in a four-in-hand. Everything was of the finest and most elegant, and, incidentally, the most costly to be had in the whole city.

Perhaps he was a little homesick, lonely, as he stood on the deck of his boat, watching the shore recede, watching his faithful comrades wave to him until he was out of sight. Probably his eyes were moist. Little did he realize, any more than Whistler had, that he was to live abroad all the rest of his days. However, unlike Whistler, he was to return several times to visit America, and he was to do some great pieces of work, which were commissioned by his country. Although he was to live abroad, he was to passionately cling to his Americanism and to toil hard for his homeland!

He was eager to go to the haunts of Shakespeare when he arrived in England, and set out at once for Stratford-on-Avon. His first home was there, and the very room he occupied had once been our Washington Irving's! Irving had gone to England many years before on a similar quest to Abbey's—to seek the right atmosphere to write of "Old England." In this room he had written his celebrated *Bracebridge Hall* and *An Old English Christmas*. The two Americans were very much alike (Washington Irving had died when Abbey was seven), for they were both generous, gentle, and humorous, and they both loved the England of the seventeenth century. Abbey wrote a description of his room in a letter home:

"My little parlor is cozy—it is larger than Irving said! There is a bright fire burning in the grate, the same grate he poked at! His chair is in the corner with a brass label at the back to say so. On the walls are quantities of framed prints and souvenirs of Irving. At the windows there are red curtains and Venetian blinds. Of course, there is a Manx cat purring on the hearth—a Manx cat without a tail" (a descendant of a Manx cat which had once lain on Washington Irving's hearth).

Whistler was living in England at this time. Abbey admired him very much, and went down to visit him at his famous "White House" in Chelsea. There was another celebrated American artist in England (whose story is still to be told)—John Singer Sargent. Sargent and Abbey became very great friends and worked together for many years.

On one of Abbey's brief visits to America he met a Miss Mead, a very charming and cultured American who knew a great deal about art. She was a graduate of Vassar and had traveled a great deal abroad, studying the language and literature of France and Germany. Not only this, but she was an expert swimmer and a splendid horsewoman. For a while she taught in the Roxbury Latin School, to prove that she could earn her own living. A very fine type of American woman! A beautiful friendship grew between this Miss Mead and Abbey, and two years after their first meeting they were married. Their marriage was a very happy one, for between them was a perfect understanding and sympathy.

Abbey's fame was steadily growing. He was now ready to open a studio of his own in England. For a while after he was married he and his wife traveled about, seeking for the perfect place for a home and a spot for a studio. This studio had to be large, for he had become interested in mural painting, and murals are much larger than most paintings, for they are not framed and hung, but are intended to decorate a ceiling or a definite wall space. The early mural painters worked right on the plastered walls or ceilings. Michelangelo, for instance, lay for months on his back as he painted the ceiling of the Sistine Chapel, while paint dripped into his eyes and over his beard. The modern mural painter paints on a canvas, which is later glued to the wall or ceiling for which it is intended. Thus they are spared a stiff neck (that was Michelangelo's misery).

A mural painter plans his work with the architect of the building. The architect decides that this or that wall should be decorated. The artist then selects a story which will be appropriate for the building, or the town in which the building stands. The mural must be, of course, in perfect harmony with the building in color and design. American mural painters had learned much from the Italians and the French, but they did not copy them.

Abbey built his great studio on a beautiful estate in the heart of the English countryside he loved so well. He and his wife found a wonderful spot to make their home in the quaint old town of Fairport, which was noted for the stained-glass windows in the church. "Morgan Hall," as his home was called, was a lovely, serene old house, with a walled garden, fine old trees, and a wide meadow beyond. The house had been built in the days of knighthood and chivalry, and about it clung memories of those romantic days that Abbey cherished. In this charming place Mr. and Mrs. Abbey were delightful hosts, and its doors were always open to American artists abroad.

The studio itself was very large, the largest in all Europe, for it was sixty-four feet long and forty feet wide. In such a studio Abbey could build the huge frame for his murals and set a stage upon which his models could pose. There was a marvelous wardrobe; no theatrical wardrobe could be more magnificent; for hanging in rows and rows were gorgeous costumes of every imaginable hue, and suits of shining armor! What a brilliant display it must have been, for there were robes of great splendor that might have been worn at the Court of King Arthur or that of Good Queen Bess! If all the princes and princesses of fairy tales and all the knights and ladies of our great legends had come a-visiting this studio at Fairport, they would not have needed to bring their trunks! Mrs. Abbey, whose task it was to take care of this wonderful wardrobe, could have fitted them all out for an extended stay!

The year 1890 was an important one for Abbey, for he was made a member of the Royal Academy, an honor England gives to her greatest artists. In this same year the famous architects in America, McKim, Mead & White, were planning the Boston Library, and they wanted American artists to decorate the interior. They asked Whistler, Sargent, and Abbey to do the murals. Whistler felt he was getting too old, and so he refused. Sargent and Abbey worked on their murals side by side at Fairport, each artist taking a different story for his decoration.

Abbey chose his favorite legend, one that he considered the most beautiful of English legends, "The Quest of the Holy Grail." It is a story beloved and known to boys and girls the world over, the story of Sir Galahad, the stainless youth of King Arthur's Court, who, because his heart was pure, hoped to see the "Holy Grail," the cup from which Christ drank at the Last Supper.

These murals consist of fifteen panels which continue from one to the other the experiences of Sir Galahad in his holy quest. Sir Galahad is pictured in a deep rich red, instead of white, as he most usually is. Red, to Abbey, stood for a purity that had been tried and proved; to him it was a stronger color than white. All of these panels are rich and glowing in color, and harmonize beautifully with the black walnut wood-work of the room. This lovely warm red that Abbey used in these murals was always one of his favorite colors.

What a wonderful time they had, Sargent and Abbey working side by side in the great studio at Fairport, and how much it delighted them, this commission to make beautiful a New England city! Although they were living abroad, no task made them more happy than working for America! After painting all day, they spent many happy evenings together—Sargent, Mrs. Abbey, and her very gracious and charming old mother who had come to live with them. Sargent delighted them with his music. Four more congenial companions it would be hard to imagine!

Although Abbey received great commissions from England, for he was asked to paint the coronation of King Edward VII, his devotion and loyalty to America and American artists grew deeper as time went on. Everything that touched America or American artists touched him. Another very noted American mural painter, Edwin Blashfield, and Abbey wrote many letters about the future American mural painters. Abbey was very much interested in building a hotel for American artists living abroad, for he felt that if Americans lived together they would keep more American, even if they were living on foreign soil.

There were now many young American sculptors, architects, and painters in Europe, who had won scholarships from the big colleges. All of the great universities—Harvard, Columbia, Pennsylvania, and many others—were doing all they could to inspire the artists of America. American artists were now doing splendid work.

Abbey passionately loved the history of his native state, and he was deeply proud and happy when he was asked to paint the murals of her state Capitol at Harrisburg. No task ever asked of him filled him with such sincere emotion, for he was grateful to be permitted to do a service for his native state and pay a tribute to his countrymen. He did not dream that it was to be his last work and that he would never live to finish it.

One day in 1908 Abbey stood, brush in hand, in his great studio at Fairport, looking down at a huge packing-box. He had just finished painting in an address. His eyes were filled with pride, affection, and a little of the quiet humor that was so a part of him. The address was brief; at a glance it seemed incomplete. Had he something else to write? No, he had finished. All that was written on the huge packing-box was "The Commonwealth of Pennsylvania."

It was the supreme task of his life, the finest thing that he had done—these murals for the Harrisburg state Capitol. They tell the history of the state and pay a tribute to all the things which helped to make it great and powerful. In his painting called "Religious Liberty" his tribute is to William Penn, who opened wide the doors of this community to the people of all creeds. This noble and inspiring subject was his choice for his first mural. After this were paintings which showed what coal, oil, and steel had meant to Penn's Commonwealth. The whole glorious history of Pennsylvania was all here, from the supreme toil of man to the grandeur and wonder of God!

Neither Mrs. Abbey nor Abbey dreamed of the catastrophe that was ahead of them. Abbey was painting these splendid murals with all the intensity and passion of his nature. His heart and soul were wrapped up in his work. On one beautiful day in the year 1911 he was visiting friends. He was not well, but he never for one moment took his health seriously and tried to forget his feelings. Mrs. Abbey was worried and sent for one of the most famous doctors in England. To their surprise, he ordered an operation at once. "No, no!" Abbey said. "I've too much work to do and I feel well enough to do it." He refused to believe that anything was seriously wrong and insisted upon keeping his appointments; he was eager and anxious to see his friends. Mrs. Abbey cabled to America for a noted surgeon. The operation was at last performed; it was too late, there was no hope. The great painter had only a few weeks more. Abbey was not told, and he believed that it was only the heat of an unusually warm June that made him so weak. He delighted in the flowers and notes which his friends sent him because he was ill, but he went on planning his work as though he were soon to be up and about.

They carried his bed into his great studio, so that he

could lie and study his painting called "Valley Forge," which was one of the Harrisburg murals. He himself was in another valley—the Valley of the Shadow of Death— but he did not know it. His hands were eager for his brushes, he longed to be at his work. His eyes closed, his hands lay still. His supreme work, his mighty work, was unfinished. The end had come, this clear, radiant August day. England's greatest paid their tribute to the departed artist, as also did the highest representatives of his native land, for the American ambassador, Whitelaw Reid, was there at Golder's Green on August 3, 1911, when the mortal remains of Edwin Austin Abbey were cremated. His immortal self—the self that would live forever among people—was in his monument, done with his own hands— a monument which everlastingly glorified his beloved Pennsylvania in the state Capitol at Harrisburg!

VII

AUGUSTUS SAINT GAUDENS

America's Greatest Sculptor

N THE QUAINT LITTLE FRENCH
VILLAGE OF ASPET, AT THE FOOT
OF THE PYRENEES, WAS A FAM-
ILY OF SHOEMAKERS, WHOSE
NAME WAS SAINT GAUDENS.
For generations they had plied their trade, and each generation had improved upon the last until, under one Bernard
Paul Ernest Saint Gaudens, they were shoemakers on a
large scale. Aspet is in the province of Gascony, a French
province near the Spanish border. The Gascons, in story
and art, were celebrated for their daring, their love of adventure, and the picturesque manner in which they boasted
and bragged of their experiences. In telling a tale they let
their imaginations run riot, for a tale was utterly useless
and stupid to them unless it was highly entertaining. A
story *was* a story and truth was the truth, and there was no
reason at all why they should be the same thing. Maybe
the Gascons *were* known for braggart adventurers, but
what gorgeous yarns they could tell! Imagine the fish story
of Gascon fishermen if you can! Yards long—several feet—
big pearly teeth and long eye lashes and what not, they
most likely would have given to the fish caught in their

streams. Perhaps you have heard of a bold and dashing Gascon named D'Artagnan, the romantic hero of *The Three Musketeers*. There are many books filled with the tales of the imaginative Gascon!

Bernard Paul Ernest Saint Gaudens was a Gascon to his finger tips, or better, to the tip of his tongue, for from it rolled the most lavish and fantastic tales ever heard in Gascony. This vivid imagination he gave as a precious gift to his son Augustus, quite untarnished. Augustus was not to use it on shoes or story-telling, but with it and the aid of his long slender fingers he was to create things of everlasting beauty. He was to be America's greatest sculptor, one of her supremely great artists.

Just how the title "Saint" came to the family and just why there was a town in Gascony by that name was one of Bernard Paul Ernest's favorite tales. He told it so often that he came at last to believe it as Gospel truth. There was, he said, in Rome a master architect by the name of "Gaudens." This architect designed and planned the mighty Colosseum, which was, of course, a task of extreme greatness. But, alas! this "Gaudens" was a pagan, believing in a troop of gods and goddesses. To celebrate the completion of this tremendous work, in a proper and more holy spirit, he decided to become a Christian, and not only a Christian, but a Christian martyr. He desired to be cast before lions in the arena of his Colosseum, and so spill his blood as a noble sacrifice upon his own altar. For this he was made a saint, and in the course of time a town in Gascony was named for him. This was Bernard Paul Ernest

Saint Gaudens's story, and a story he stuck to through thick and thin, regardless of the fact that there was nothing on earth to prove that one word of it was true.

A legend, as perhaps you know, is a story that has been told over and over for generations, in just the same way— a story that may or may not be true. There was a legend about the town of Saint Gaudens which had been told for centuries—a legend very different from Bernard's. The other story runs like this: One day in the fifth century a young shepherd boy was watching his flocks, and as he watched he reverently repeated his prayers. Some Saracens, or wandering Arabs, who were the bitter enemies of the early Christians, crossed the Spanish Pyrenees with the intention of slaying any Christians in their path. When they came upon the young shepherd they made fun of him for praying, and insisted that he change his faith. The boy repeated courageously and sturdily his faith in God, and at last one of the Saracens in a fury drew his scimitar and promptly cut off the boy's head. But the boy, instead of falling down on the ground, picked up his head in his hands and ran to the small church near by. The Saracen was at first too amazed to move, and then in a mad fury jumped upon his horse and dashed after the boy. The young shepherd had just time to close the door of the church after him when the Saracen and his horse beat themselves against it. To this day it is said that the marks of the horse's hoofs can be seen on the church door! This child was called "Gaudens," and as he died for his faith he was made a saint, and so a town was called Saint Gaudens in his honor.

Bernard Paul Ernest Saint Gaudens's story of his family name may be very different from this old legend, but it had one very striking and interesting detail to it—he wanted the first of his name to be a master artist, the architect of the Colosseum; and when he told his story he little realized that his own son was to be a master artist and work in stone that never perishes! A Saint Gaudens was to be a supreme master artist, but fortunately he was to work in a country that never asks any one to die for his faith.

Bernard Saint Gaudens, with the rest of his family, left their native village and moved on to another town. He and his older brother had a huge shoemaking establishment in this new town, for they employed thirty or forty workmen. You see, they did not just mend shoes, as most of our shoemakers do today; they actually made them. Bernard grew restless and longed for new worlds to conquer with his shoes, and finally he left France and went to London, and then on to Dublin. In the shoe shop in Dublin in which he worked was a pretty young Irish girl, with curly black hair, clear skin, a generous loving mouth, and a pair of warm blue eyes. She was binding slippers all day long. Her people had been plasterers—in fact, plasterers ran in her family as shoemakers ran in the Saint Gaudens family. In those days a family passed a trade on as a matter of course to the next generation. Mary McGuinness, for that was the name of this pretty girl who bound slippers, was probably very much impressed with the dashing, red-haired Gascon, working in her shop, for he was certainly captivated with her. "The most beautiful girl in the world" was what he called her. She taught him a very remarkable English, for his fierce French accent was mixed with a rich Irish brogue. For seven years he worked at her side, toiling for her for seven years, just as Jacob in the Bible toiled for Rachel, before they could marry. Those seven years seemed "as a day because of the love he bore her."

Two sons were born to them who died as infants. Then when their third son, Augustus, was only six months old a fearful famine swept over Ireland. They looked tragically at each other and then at their precious baby, and in a terror that it too might be taken from them, they decided to leave Ireland. Beyond the ocean, America beckoned them, held out hope. Had the famine come six months earlier, America's greatest sculptor would have been born on her shores.

Even about this sad departure Bernard had a tale to tell. He wanted it more tragic—or more nearly tragic than it was. He always said that he had tried to get passage on a ship named *Star of the West*, but he could not, as the passenger list was overcrowded. Had they taken this ship, they would all have been burned at sea and so would have come to a horrible end. It pleased Bernard's imagination to think how nearly they had come to a melodramatic death. He enjoyed, as he told this story, watching his listeners shiver at the near escape from a ghastly tragedy.

The tall Gascon and his sweet-faced Irish wife, with her baby at her breast, arrived in Boston some time in September, 1848—the baby had been born on March 1st, six months before. Bernard left his young wife and infant son in Boston, and went to New York City to seek work and find a home for his little family. Six weeks later he sent for her. Their first real home in America was down in Houston Street. By a strange and interesting coincidence, this very building they lived in was to become a bronze foundry, the very foundry in which one of Augustus Saint Gaudens's greatest statues was to be cast!

Of course Bernard Saint Gaudens went in for shoes, because it was the only trade he knew. And what original ideas and notions he had, too, of how shoes should be made! He most certainly used his Gascon daring and imagination to a lavish extent upon them. It is a marvel that his business continued to thrive as it did, for he had among his customers some very prominent families, including that of the Governor and some of the Astors and the Belmonts. He remained perfectly serene and undisturbed when they came limping back to him, complaining that they were in agony. He made those shoes right, and if they hurt, it certainly was not his fault or concern. Their feet were all wrong and nothing at all was wrong with his shoemaking. Perhaps it was this calm assurance that he was right that made them come again and again, or perhaps it was because he advertised as a "French shoemaker," and French shoes were considered "very smart" and were all the rage. His customers, very likely, were fascinated by his extraordinary personality. He had many curious expressions, which he used in that fantastic accent, part French, part Irish. These expressions amused and delighted his customers. For instance, he always spoke of anything useless as "much use as a mustard plaster on a wooden leg." One of his favorite remarks all his days was, "What you are saying and nothing at all is the same thing."

Besides his very independent way of making shoes, he had one other trait which interfered with a nice smooth business career. He loved to belong to societies, several at a time, and nothing would do but he must rule them. As his son Augustus once said, he must be the "Grand Panjamdrum," or, as we might say, the "High Mucky Muck." In the daytime when he might have been making shoes he was often writing long and remarkable letters, with big flourishes of his pen, to the members of these various societies. His wife often gently pleaded with him to remember that there were a few shoe orders to fill, but he would wave her aside good-naturedly and continue with great gusto to finish his letter-writing.

Augustus Saint Gaudens's life in the Bowery, as a boy, was like that of thousands of boys brought up on city streets, among the docks, smoke, soot, chimneys, and horse-cars, and under the elevated trains! It doesn't seem just the place for a boy to dream of being an artist, does it? In after-years when he was abroad he sometimes grew homesick and longed for the street scenes and street smells of his childhood. He belonged, he said, to America. There was his home, there he wanted to be, with the "elevated train dropping oil and ashes on the idiot below, the cable cars, telegraph poles"—all had become very dear to him.

From dark, dingy streets in the heart of the city has risen many a great leader and many a genius! And the true story of their lives is more inspiring than that of the hero of some fairy tale or fable.

The young Saint Gaudens played all the street games, indulged in all the pranks that any city boy does. One of his favorite tricks was, with some friends, to stretch a string from some stoop, to the top of a wagon standing at the curb. This game was played in the dark, so the string did not show. The boys hid near by, waiting with impish glee to hear the hats roll off into the gutter as some unsuspecting man walked himself and a derby in under the string. This game was not intended for policemen, but once in a while, by chance, a policeman did stride along unsuspectingly! But when, from their hiding-places, the boys saw and heard a policeman's cap roll into the street, what a gorgeous and unholy delight filled their souls as with a whispered, "Cheese it!" they dashed for safety! Besides this sport, the boys often "swiped" sweet potatoes from a push-cart, to cook in an oven built out of cobblestones. In the evening they occasionally crept into the old graveyard near by, and picked the flowers, simple little weeds, among the graves, for they were the only flowers in the whole neighborhood.

Augustus Saint Gaudens was not fond of school (which, alas! so many boys share with him, that it does not mean that they are to be great). He especially hated being sent to the Moore Street school. Of this school he had no tender memories. His memories were mostly of "being kept in," and many, too many "lickings." He remembered always the street fights, to and from school and after school, between "his gang" and the other fellows' "gang." Names and stones flew in all directions. Sometimes the boys daringly charged up the enemies' street, to defend, as they claimed, "Lady Washington's White Ghost" (not that they ever saw her, or cared much for her, but she was as good an excuse as any for a good fight). On such occasions a right royal fist battle was sure to follow. Of course, like many boys, young Saint Gaudens had a faithful yellow cur at his heels, which followed him through all his trials and troubles.

The boy Saint Gaudens especially hated one of his teachers at the Moore Street school—Pop Belden, as the boys called him. On one occasion, after a big commotion in the classroom, Augustus was sent to the corner and ordered to turn his face to the blackboard. The boy found the blackboard about as stupid and uninteresting as anything could be, and so he decided to amuse himself, with the few things at hand, such as chalk and eraser. He smeared the eraser with chalk dust, and then very carefully wiped it over his face. The teacher's back was turned (he made sure of that), and, eager to share this amusement with his classmates, he turned and faced them with a broad grin. Of course there was instantly a wild uproarious shout of pure joy from the class. It meant, alas! another afternoon after school, another afternoon sitting forlornly in his seat, with the happy shouts of his playmates coming up from the streets through the windows to mock him in his misery.

The only part of the school day that the boy enjoyed was recess. Were it not for recesses on school days, and his occasional trips on Sundays to New Jersey, he would have felt his school days were utterly wretched.

It was at the Moore Street school that he first showed his talent and interest in drawing. His earliest recollections of drawing were more amusing than serious. He remembered drawing in chalk two regiments of soldiers facing each other, firing right into each other's faces. Great clouds of smoke almost hid them from view. As he looked proudly upon this masterpiece he let out a little shout of joy and with his chalk added more and more clouds of smoke, for the battle was getting hotter each moment. In the end nothing was left of the drawing, for it went right up in smoke. On another occasion, while visiting in the country, he drew all over the walls of a clean white house, a drawing that far from pleased his hostess! His most difficult and ambitious painting in those early years was on a fence in a back yard. It was a Negro boy with a hole in the knee of his trousers, through which the knee itself showed. This boy was holding in his hand a target. The young artist, after he had completed his work of art, took a bow and arrow and amused himself seeing how near he could come to the bull's-eye. In this way he made his painting serve two loves—that of drawing and that of marksmanship. He paid rather heavily for any joy he received from this painting, for it was followed with a fearful and wonderful attack of the "colly-wobbles," due to the fact that he used saliva in mixing the paint, instead of water.

However, there was some one—a customer of his father's, a Dr. Cornelius Rea Agnew—who took these early drawings seriously and recognized the boy's talent. One day, on visiting the shoe shop, he found Augustus Saint Gaudens making a very remarkable drawing of his father's shoemakers at work. He stopped and asked the boy if he wanted to be an artist. When the boy answered, "Yes," Dr. Rea Agnew urged the boy's father to permit him to follow his heart's desire.

The boy's school days were nearly over, and, fortunately, before he gave up school forever he had a brief period of going to a school where he was happy. The Saint Gaudenses had moved, and so he left the Moore Street school district. In this new school he was never punished, and he dearly loved his teacher. It is good to feel that he could remember that all schools are not hard and miserable places!

After school he usually did errands for his father in the afternoon, delivering shoes. This meant going through the "enemies' country," and often in the fight that followed he lost a shoe. Bernard Saint Gaudens began to feel that his son's childhood and school days must end. The boy was thirteen! One day he said:

"My boy, you must go to work. What would you like to do?"

"I don't care," he replied, "but I should like it if I could do something which would help me to be an artist."

Like several of the artists of whom we have read, Augustus Saint Gaudens was apprenticed to learn a trade. From the very first he preferred to use a chisel and cut stone, rather than use a brush, and so his father had him apprenticed to a man named Avet, who was a stone cameo cutter. In those days it was considered most elegant to wear stone cameo scarf-pins, with heads of dogs, horses, and lions cut in amethyst or other stone. Avet was the first stone cameo cutter in America, and he often did work for one of the finest jewelry firms—Tiffany's.

Saint Gaudens remembered his years of apprenticeship, as Winslow Homer had, as miserable years of slavery. Avet came from the province of Savoy. He was a dark, swarthy man, with a huge mustache. He had a violent and ferocious temper, and he howled at the boy continuously. However, when he was not shrieking out complaints, he was singing at the top of his lungs, in a voice that fairly bellowed. It would be hard to say which was harder to stand!

Saint Gaudens had to be at his shop at seven o'clock, and he lived a long way from it. He hated, like most boys, trudging along so early in the morning, so he often "hitched" a ride on one of the omnibuses, in order to save ten cents—and quite as often had to fight with some one who wanted to push him off the step.

In spite of Avet's stormy uncertain disposition, he often took his apprentice away on Sundays for outings to New Jersey. These trips were heavenly, for he enjoyed lying on the soft green grass on his back, looking up through the lacy green branches, upward and upward to the infinite, limitless blue! On these trips he could swim, and swimming was one of his greatest joys his whole life long.

For three and a half years Saint Gaudens slaved under the mastery of the cameo cutter Avet, and managed to withstand his storms and mighty oaths and endure his noisy, untuneful singing. During these years he saw many things outside the shop to inspire him in his longing to be a sculptor. He was overwhelmed with ecstasy and admiration when he saw John Quincy Adams Ward's "Indian Hunter." It was Adams who was his first real inspiration. Ward was twelve years older than Saint Gaudens, and in the twelve years that lay between them America had done much to encourage a young sculptor. Ward was, with a fine generosity, in later years to do something more for Saint Gaudens than merely inspire him.

One day Avet burst into the studio with a roar like thunder, stamping about, firing things this way and that. His young apprentice had not brushed up the crumbs from his lunch! He was in a fury; he discharged the boy then and there.

The poor boy, stunned, wrapped up his overalls and walked home. To him, for the moment, the end of the world had come; life held nothing. All his three and a half years were wasted; his hope of a career seemed, for the moment, dashed to pieces. He told his father the story with a heavy heart. Avet, in the meantime, had calmed down and was very sorry, for he fully recognized the value of the boy's skill. He dashed after him, burst in upon the family group, and asked Saint Gaudens to come back to him—with a five-dollar-a-week raise. But the passionate pride and courage that ran in his blood made him haughtily reject this offer. In a dramatic speech he spurned Avet's offer, although he had no idea where he was going to work next. Bernard Saint Gaudens stood by, smiling and puffed up with pride at his son's magnificent independence. It was just what he would have done under the circumstances.

Saint Gaudens was to discover that all stone cutters were not harsh task-masters any more than all schools and school-teachers were disagreeable. His next master, Jules Le Brethon, was as different from Avet as night from day. The only trait that he had like Avet's was that he, too, sang, but in a happy, joyous way, from morn until night.

During these years of apprenticeship the boy, each night after tea, went to Cooper Institute for drawing-lessons. All his life he was grateful to the teachers, to this whole school, for the help they gave him.

In later years he was to make a statue of Peter Cooper, the founder of the Institute. It was a labor of love and loyalty for the founder of the Institute that had given so much to him. This statue stands in front of Cooper Institute today, and it was this statue that was cast in the building which had been the first home of the Saint Gaudenses in America!

There was one scene in Saint Gaudens's youth that was to make a very deep and lasting impression upon him and was to come back to him very vividly in after-years. One morning he came to breakfast to find his mother and father in tears, choking with convulsive sobs. On the table before them lay an open newspaper. Its glaring and tragic headlines caught his eye and a feeling of horror and passionate grief swept over him. President Lincoln had been assassinated! A few days later he was one of the long, seemingly endless line that reverently and solemnly formed to pass before the bier of the martyred President as he lay in state at the City Hall in New York City. The boy looked upon that tragic and noble face, quiet and at peace in the majesty of death, and was stirred to the depths of his soul. Then he turned and went to the end of that long, long line, and once again slowly made his way before the bier. And so forever those noble features were to be indelibly impressed upon him. It is small wonder that the statue of Lincoln that he was to make had in it so much grandeur and sincerity.

The boy, under the kindness of his master, Le Brethon, became a terrific worker, and so formed a habit he was to have the rest of his life. After toiling hard all day, he barely snatched a supper, and rushed out again to the art school to work for a few more hours.

One day his father asked him, quite casually, but with a sly smile, how he would like to go to the Paris Exposition. The father relished the dramatic effect of this question. Just as though there could be any doubt as to the answer! *"How would he like to go to Paris?"* The boy was jubilant, in seventh heaven. Yes! Yes! "Perhaps," his father half promised, "we can arrange it!" He knew very well it was to be arranged, but he enjoyed, as many fathers do, a little teasing.

The trip was to be a turning-point in the boy's life. He

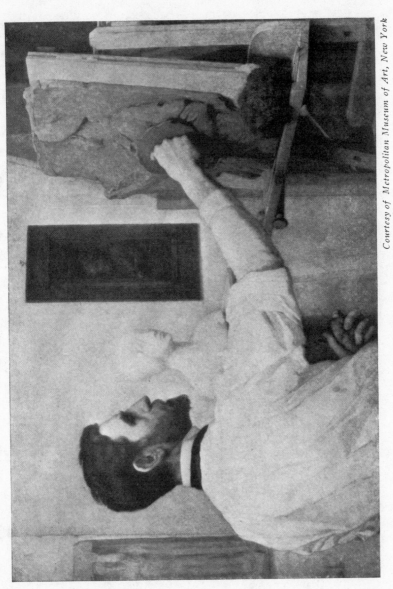

AUGUSTUS SAINT GAUDENS *by* KENYON COX

was not nineteen, and his whole heart was wrapped up in his art. Sometimes, as he was jostled and pushed about on a horse-car or a bus, he thought to himself "if they only knew, for they are crowding, shoving, and pushing about one who is to be a great artist, one who is to be famous." Very clearly he saw his own particular bright and shining star, to which he was hitching his wagon!

His departure for Paris was celebrated with several elaborate dinners. His good-natured generous father arranged one very festive and hilarious affair for him. The kindly Le Brethon did the same. As he raised his napkin, the night of his last banquet, he found one hundred francs in shining gold! With it was a note saying they were for a visit to his father's birthplace at Aspet, France. Just before he went away, he made a bust of his father, and a drawing of his mother. It was a heartache to him, later on in after-years, that these were both completely destroyed in a fire in his studio.

The boy crossed over in the steerage, and the whole trip to him was one long nightmare, for he said he was not as sick as a dog, but as a "whole regiment of dogs." After visiting his father's relatives for a short time, he had to search for work, for one of his uncles had been down on his luck and the boy had helped him, out of his small fortune. He found work with a cameo cutter, an Italian named Lupi, who lived in the picturesque Latin Quarter, and it was here the boy came to live.

In the mornings he attended a modeling-school, for his ambition to become a sculptor was now intense; in the afternoons he supported himself with his cameo cutting. He worked so much harder on his modeling than on his cameo cutting, that he became miserably, wretchedly poor. He barely earned enough to keep himself alive, and for a while his only bed was a mattress on the floor. His struggle for success had become so grim and cruel that it made him very serious and silent—made him forget that there were gay times to be had in the lively Latin Quarter.

He longed with all his heart to take lessons at the Beaux Arts, the best art school in Paris. But it was not a simple matter. He appealed to the American ambassador to help him, and the ambassador promised to aid the young American, who was sure of becoming a great sculptor. However, it was nine long weary months before he was admitted, and in the meantime he attended a small art school. This school was overcrowded and the room in which he worked was dark and stuffy. Here he modeled from a nude model, which was to be a great help to him later on. His work in this school was rewarded, for he received their first prize, a medal, which was a crown of laurel. After nine months of hard work one day he received a huge envelope with the United States seal upon it. His joy was beyond description, his spirits were soaring, for he was to be admitted to the Beaux Arts. He was the first American artist to be granted this privilege, but in six months another was to follow, and then many more!

It does seem strange that a boy whose father was French and mother Irish (both so light-hearted) should be so sternly above ordinary simple pleasures, living as he was in the gay Latin Quarter. There was something of the Spartan about him, for he endured his poverty without a complaint. All the rest of his life he was known as a silent, austere man, for, although he had a sense of humor, he was never frivolous or very talkative. He took his work very seriously. And why not? A sculptor's work lasts forever, and he considered it a crime to do something in stone, to be plastered up in front of the world to last for centuries, that might be a disgrace. A bad painting, he said, could be taken down off a wall and put in an attic, but statues out in public places are stuck there for ages.

After he had studied in Paris for three years, he went to Rome. For this longed-for visit he had to borrow money from his brother. The beauty and grandeur of ancient Rome enthralled him, and he felt, as he went into the Eternal City, as though he were entering Paradise!

And here, as in Paris, he had to continue his cameo cutting to keep himself alive. His master in Rome was one of the finest in the city, and he paid Saint Gaudens sufficiently well, so that he might take a studio of his own. All about him were the masterpieces of supreme artists to inspire him, but with great strength of character and originality he chose a subject for his first statue that could never in the world have been dreamed of by an Italian—Hiawatha! Hiawatha, the young Indian boy, musing, brooding in the heart of America's primeval forest, immortalized in stone, in the heart of ancient Rome! Saint Gaudens was like the greatest of the Italian sculptors—he was independent. So easily he might have copied, or been influenced by the beautiful work about him, but, like the supreme artists, he never copied. A wealthy American visiting in Rome—a Montgomery Gibbs—advanced him the money to cast his statue of Hiawatha. Later on, this statue was bought by Governor Morgan of New York.

After three years in Rome, Saint Gaudens was very ill with Roman fever. His good friend, Montgomery Gibbs, once more came to his aid and gave him the money to return to America. After his years abroad, he was longing to see America, longing to see his own people again. You can imagine the wild shouts of joy that greeted his sudden and unexpected appearance in his father's shop one day. His parents were overwhelmed with pride and happiness. It was not for long that he was to stay home, for he made another visit to Rome. As he waved good-by to his mother and father, his heart was heavy with fear and a strange apprehension possessed him. He felt as though he would never again see that good, sweet face of his mother. And he never did, for she was to die before he returned again to America.

His fortunes were steadily improving, and for a while he was very happy with the companionship of some very delightful Italian families. On this visit to Rome he also made the friendship of a charming American, a Miss Augusta Homer. She always remembered one visit he made to her in the pouring rain. Because, for the moment, his heart was light, good fortune was promised to him, and he was soon to see the one girl in all the world, he bought some elaborate clothes, topped with the most extraordinary high and shining silk hat imaginable. In this costume he gayly marched across the square with the rain beating against him—and no umbrella.

His days of cameo cutting were numbered. In a short time he would not need it to keep him alive. His last "cameo" was an all-important one, for it was set in an engagement ring for Augusta Homer. For there was soon to be an Augusta, as well as an Augustus, Saint Gaudens.

On his return to America, after this visit, he found his fortune had indeed changed. Orders came to him in dazzling and marvelous rapidity. He was told that there was wanted a statue of Admiral Farragut, and he was asked to apply for this commission. The dean of American sculptors, the most eminent and prominent sculptor in the city, John Quincy Adams Ward, was also considered for this work. If Saint Gaudens received this commission it would be by the skin of his teeth. He was new and untried. Ward had made his name. However, Ward, with a fine generous spirit, withdrew in favor of the young sculptor and did everything within his power to see that Saint Gaudens received the commission. The vote had stood nearly even; now it was all in Saint Gaudens's favor. His joy knew no bounds; he leaped for joy at this wonderful opportunity.

And today, as one drives up Fifth Avenue, he may see, as he passes Madison Square, the figure of Admiral Farragut, the great American sailor, standing on his pedestal, as though he were on the deck of his good ship. The Admiral stands perfectly still; his hands are not raised. He

is in a quiet dignified pose, the pose of a strong commander—a commander that was every inch a man!

The pedestal upon which the Admiral is standing is
considered one of the finest things of its kind in America,
and it was designed by Saint Gaudens's warm personal
friend, the noted American architect, Stanford White.
In making this statue of Farragut the sculptor also made
his name and fame. From the time it was finished until
he died he had so many commissions that he always had
to work on several at once.

In New York City is another wonderful example of this
sculptor's genius. It is the statue of General Sherman which
stands at the south entrance to Central Park at Fifty-ninth
Street and Fifth Avenue. General Sherman is on his horse;
before him is the figure of Victory, leading him on his way.
A famous American artist and critic, Kenyon Cox, said
this statue of General Sherman is the third greatest eques-
trian statue in the world. The other two which he considered greater were done by Italian sculptors—Verrocchio
and Donatello. After Saint Gaudens had died, Kenyon
Cox said that he was not at all sure that this statue of
Saint Gaudens's was not in its own way equal to the statues
of these masters. The "General Sherman" was exhibited
in Paris, and was hailed as the work of a genius. The
French gave Saint Gaudens their highest distinctions and
made him an officer of the Legion of Honor! It would seem
that the French agreed with Kenyon Cox as to the greatness of this statue! Incidentally, Kenyon Cox painted a
picture of Saint Gaudens which hangs in the Metropolitan

Museum of Art, which shows the sculptor working on the head of another famous American painter, William M. Chase.

Is it any wonder that Saint Gaudens should have been thrilled by the progress of American artists, and by the honors paid to an American in a country that had an art long before America was even discovered? American artists were now doing splendid work and it made him proud and happy. He returned from Paris after his "Sherman" had been exhibited, saying: "I am coming home a red-hot patriot. My visit has made me feel that we Americans can stand on our own feet artistically."

The great sculptor toiled unceasingly. His spirit never waned, although his body began to weaken under the strain of long hours of hard work. His face was very weary at times, and as some one once said, "it was full of a pathetic charm like that of a weary lion." His hair and beard were of the same tawny hue as the mane of a lion, which perhaps helped to give this impression. The last ten years of Saint Gaudens's life were a long, bitter struggle against ill-health, with death always facing him. Regardless of this, he never ceased to accept commissions, never ceased to work toward the goal of glorious perfection. He was never satisfied with his work, always felt that it could be and must be better. Great men never seem to realize how fine their work is. Lincoln felt depressed as he finished his immortal Gettysburg speech, felt that it had been a failure!

On one of Saint Gaudens's visits to Paris he met and came to know Whistler. Whistler often stopped in at Saint

Gaudens's studio in the dusk to talk intimately with the great American sculptor. Saint Gaudens thought him a most remarkable man. On one occasion Whistler found the sculptor in a jubilant mood.

"I've just stuck up one of my things in the exhibition and I am feeling somewhat cocky about it," Saint Gaudens said.

"That's the way to feel," Whistler jerked out. "That's the way," and then continued, with great energy, "If you ever feel otherwise, never admit it, never admit it."

To Saint Gaudens this showed the bravery of Whistler, his refusal to ever admit that life hurt or disappointed him. Saint Gaudens was proud to be asked in later years, after Whistler's death, to make the plaque of Whistler which is at West Point.

Another intimate friendship of Saint Gaudens's life was that of Robert Louis Stevenson. Robert Louis Stevenson is the author of many a wonderful tale of high adventure— for what boy or girl, for that matter, has not delighted in *Treasure Island?*—and he did most of his writing on the flat of his back, for he was an incurable invalid. Saint Gaudens, whose own health was breaking when he met Stevenson, was deeply touched and impressed by the author's great bravery and gentleness in the face of certain death. Saint Gaudens had at first found it hard to be reconciled to never being a robust, healthy man again, and the example set by Stevenson inspired and helped him. Stevenson was very fond of Saint Gaudens and called him his "God-like sculptor." One of the best things the sculptor

LINCOLN *by* Augustus Saint Gaudens

ever did was a *bas-relief* of Stevenson. It is no wonder he did this well—this picture in stone which is modeled low (*bas* means low)—for his years of cameo cutting were splendid training for just this sort of thing. This *bas-relief* is now in Edinburgh, Scotland.

Saint Gaudens spent the last seven years of his life in Cornish, New Hampshire. Here he had a lovely home, which he called Aspet, after his father's birthplace in France. These years in Cornish were years of hard work in spite of the fact that they were years of long-drawn-out suffering, in spite of the fact that he knew that death could be his only release. Perhaps the memory of Stevenson's courage in the face of death helped to make him patient and happy. Toward the end he grew too weak to walk or to use his hands, and he had to be carried across his gardens to the studio, where he gave orders to his assistants who were carrying out his plans. His weakness was only of the body, for his spirit was undaunted; his vision and passion for beauty deepened with his pain.

The list of the work done by this master sculptor is a very long one. His genius has glorified many a city both at home and abroad. We have spoken of his "Sherman," his "Farragut," and "Peter Cooper" in New York City; his Stevenson in Edinburgh. In Dublin there is his statue of the great Irish patriot, Parnell. Boston has his splendid statute of the great preacher, Phillips Brooks, and also the Shaw Memorial—a memorial to a young Union officer who led a colored troop into battle. Springfield has his noble "Puritan," and Chicago his statue of Lincoln. In the Rock Creek Cemetery in Washington, D. C., is the Adams Memorial, and many consider this his masterpiece. This supremely beautiful bronze statue is sometimes called "Grief," sometimes called "Death," but the most fitting name for it is the "Peace of God." This shrouded, silent figure with downcast eyes is a rare work of art, and about it is the mystery of the ages.

Great honors came to the sculptor from every side. The French had made him an officer of the Legion of Honor, the English made him a member of the Royal Academy. In Rome there is a marble tablet to mark the place where he had lived and worked. At the Pan-American Exposition held in Buffalo in 1901, American artists had made a splendid showing, for in those twenty-five years since the Centennial in Philadelphia a wonderful progress had been made. At this Exposition America gave to Augustus Saint Gaudens a special medal of honor as her greatest artist!

Perhaps the most interesting and unusual honor came to the sculptor years after his death, in 1920, an honor which he shared, in a measure, with Abraham Lincoln. A copy was made of his statue of Lincoln—a statue whose simple dignity and nobility show the humble tenderness of the Great Emancipator. This copy of Saint Gaudens's statue was presented to England to commemorate the hundred years of peace between the two countries. The statue has often been called "the glorification of the common man." And so, the "Glorified Common Man," immortalized in stone by a man of humble birth, stands today just across the way from Westminster Abbey, where the mighty and noble in English history lie buried!

Augustus Saint Gaudens on one summer day in August, 1907, lay looking out over the beautiful mountains from his beloved home, Aspet, in Cornish, New Hampshire. For a long time he had been silent. Then at last he said, quietly, "It is very beautiful, but I want to go farther away."

To us who lived after him he has not gone very far away; his spirit is with us still, his work lives forever; for he is not gone, but "departed"—for the artist never dies!

VIII

JOSEPH PENNELL

A Famous American Etcher

OH, WHAT A COUNTRY THIS IS, THIS AMERICA OF OURS! WE HAVE JUST READ THE LIFE OF A GREAT AMERICAN, ONE OF WHOSE PARENTS WAS BORN IN France, the other in Ireland, and he himself came to America as a baby in the arms of his immigrant mother. His boyhood was spent in the crowded, noisy streets of New York City—a boyhood filled with fights, color, and excitement, day in and day out. Now we are to read of another famous American, whose people had lived here for generations and whose days were filled with peace and quiet, whose dress and homes were without color, for everything about them was sober and serene. Their voices were low as to one another they spoke their gentle "thees" and "thous." Bernard Saint Gaudens loved gay and original dress, but the parents of Joseph Pennell, of whom we are now to read, wore the somber brown or gray of the Quaker. What a contrast! And yet, these lives, which seem as far apart as the poles, were thoroughly American. America, a great broad country made up of many races, many creeds, is proud of them all, cherishes all, for each has added something to her glory.

Joseph Pennell

Joseph Pennell was born in Philadelphia in 1857, and, as his Quaker parents would say, he was born seventh month, fourth, 1857 (they gave the months and days of the weeks numbers instead of the names we use). What more appropriate day could this stanch and independent American have had for a birthday than seventh month, fourth? His birthday was that of his country's—July Fourth!

The family of Joseph Pennell had gone to Quaker meetings since there had first been Quaker meetings back in old England. An ancestor of his, Robert Pennell, founded the Society of Friends in Nottinghamshire, England, in 1684, on the third day of the fifth month. Two years later he sailed for America to join William Penn's colony in America. One of this Robert Pennell's cousins married a famous Quaker minister, Mary Morgan of Wales. When she was only thirteen she sat in a Quaker meeting over which hung an "awful silence." Tears were running down the faces of many; they were waiting for the Spirit to move them. It was to this child that the Spirit came, and she was moved with the truth. A few years later she came to America as Mary Pennell, and became well known as a minister.

Larkin Pennell, the father of the artist, Joseph Pennell, had a grandfather who had Irish blood in his veins—a John Salkeld. This John Salkeld was also a famous minister, a minister known far and wide for his vigor, fearlessness, and independence. Perhaps it was from this ancestor that Joseph Pennell inherited his own fearlessness and independence—his way of saying exactly what he thought and felt. There is an interesting story told about this John Salkeld. Once at a meeting the Quakers were sitting very still in a long silence, not because they had not been moved by the Spirit into saying something, but, alas! because they were half asleep! Suddenly John Salkeld shouted loudly over the tops of the nodding heads:

"Fire! Fire!"

"Where? Where?" called the startled voice of a sleeper, abruptly awakened.

"In Hell," John thundered, "to burn up the drowsy and unconcerned."

In later years Joseph Pennell himself was to thunder at the unconcerned—but not at a Quaker meeting!

Larkin Pennell was a teacher at the Westtown Friend's Boarding School. On seventh month, fourth, 1855, he married Rebecca A. Barton, in the old meeting house on Orange Street, Philadelphia. Theirs had been a long courtship, for Rebecca had been very delicate, too ill to think of marriage. Larkin Pennell was a patient lover, and throughout the long, peaceful courtship he wrote her quiet letters. After their marriage they moved to one of those storied houses which were so typical of old Philadelphia— a red brick house with white shutters and white marble steps. It was here that Joseph Pennell was born on seventh month, fourth, a year later. One of his aunts wrote this letter about him when he was only a few days old: "He can holler and make a big noise already, yet he sleeps most of the time." So from the first he knew how to be heard, knew how to raise his voice in protest and to get attention, just as his grandfather, Joseph Salkeld had.

Joseph Pennell's father was a quiet man, sad and silent; his mother, who had so long been ill, was very little more talkative or gay! Joseph was their only child, and had they believed in fairies (which they most certainly did not!) they might have wondered if a fairy had not exchanged their own child and left a "changeling" on their doorstep, so very different from what they might have expected was their son! At times they must have been startled, bewildered, and perhaps a little frightened as they watched this boy develop in ways so different from their own or the people about them.

On the streets near by were the homes of many Quakers, homes that looked as much alike as the costumes of the Quakers themselves. They were two-storied double houses, red bricked, substantial, and plain. Their white shutters and white doorsteps were like the white collars and cuffs of the Quaker dress. Behind each house was a tiny neat little back yard, with nicely kept garden and grass plot. Trying to outdo one's neighbors was never dreamed of, and over the entire neighborhood peace and tranquillity reigned. Within the houses one might see Quaker women in their quaint and simple gowns of brown and gray. Upon their smoothly brushed hair were snowy muslin caps, about their necks soft white fichus which were crossed demurely in front. As they sat at their knitting in quiet industry, one might hear the gentle "thees" and "thous" that dropped like sweet notes of music from their lips. Beyond this neighborhood was the bustling, noisy city of the "world's people," as they called those who were not Quakers. They themselves still lived in a City of Brotherly Love, founded by their own Quaker brother, William Penn.

The aunts and cousins of Joseph Pennell were good and kind to him. They enjoyed the visits of this "only child," sometimes lonely, who came seeking companionship away from his home, which at times must have seemed appallingly quiet. All his life he remembered one among them who filled him with the keenest delight—an Annie Wallace. It was she, strangely enough for a Quaker, who read to him tales from Hawthorne's *Wonder Book* and the *Tanglewood Tales*. The little boy was held spellbound and entranced by these wondrous tales of adventure. His breathless interest, perhaps, deceived her, as she read, for very probably she took his quietness merely for the disciplined good behavior of a little Quaker boy. Little did she realize that the glamour of these tales deeply stirred his soul and he longed passionately to be away on stirring adventures— longed to share the excitement and thrill of Ulysses or Jason. How quiet and peaceful were these readings, but what a storm they made within the restless little boy!

Perhaps it was just as well that all about Joseph was peace and quiet, for although he longed for adventures, strife, and excitement, as a child he was never strong enough to stand them. It would have been impossible for him to stand a strenuous, rough-and-tumble boyhood. He was one of those unfortunate children who manage somehow or other to have one calamity or mishap after another.

He broke his right arm, which made him left-handed all his life; then, out sleigh-riding, he broke his nose; and one summer day he was stunned by lightning, which so upset his nerves that any sudden noise made him tremble; another time, he went nearly blind, and was forced to stay in a dark room for weeks! In "doing exercises," he nearly hung himself on his back veranda. His calamities were nearly as many and as varied, as Aurelia's Unfortunate Young Man in Mark Twain's story. Aurelia was engaged to be married to a man who had to keep postponing the wedding because of mishaps—a broken leg, an eye put out, a broken arm, a scalp torn off by Indians! Joseph's parents, had they been playful, might have called him "Aurelia's Unfortunate Young Man." Besides all these misfortunes, Joseph was very thin—so thin, in fact, that the boys on the street taunted him and called him "Skinny Pennell."

In spite of all these things, Joseph Pennell was not an unhappy child. No child is who knows how to entertain himself. Besides, his parents, although they may not have understood him, were very generous with him, and gave him all the toys that any boy might wish. He had plenty of paper and crayons for drawing, rocking-horses, balloons, tool-chests, balls, and boats. His most unexpected (for a Quaker child) but most cherished plaything was a wonderful box of tin soldiers. Quakers were not, nor ever could be, soldiers, for they opposed all war. They practiced what they preached and lived the lives of peaceful men. The country was in the midst of war during Joseph's little boyhood, for the Civil War was being bitterly fought not far from Philadelphia, but the Quakers, who in their hearts felt all war was wrong, could take no part in it. It was, therefore, odd that Joseph should have so loved his tin soldiers that he relished planning battles and marching his soldiers on to victory, over which the Stars and Stripes always floated in triumph. All of his first drawings were of war. Many of these drawings have been saved, but they are not very remarkable, except for the wonderful amount of action and spirit which he put into them. His horses pranced and plunged, his soldiers charged across the pages.

The Civil War came close enough to Quaker Philadelphia for him to know that war meant something more than gay parades and brilliant charges, for on one never-to-be-forgotten occasion he came to realize that war meant bloodshed! Soldiers marching thrilled him, but the sight of a crimson pool of blood splashed upon his white doorstep by some escaped prisoner turned him sick and faint. Many times after this he saw prisoners brought through the streets. This side of war—this grim, real side—touched him deeply, for he was a very sensitive child. It must have been heart-breaking and depressing to the Quakers to have these sad war scenes in their peaceful city. Once, later on, he heard fire bells clanging and church bells ringing, heard the joyous shouts of the people and the rush of feet through the streets, and he felt the extraordinary excitement in the air, although he was not permitted to share it. The city— that is, the city of the "world's people"—had gone wild with joy over the Gettysburg victory.

Joseph Pennell's parents at last came to realize that their

little son was too much alone and that he needed the companionship of other children, so they sent him to school. Among the teachers at this school was a "Teacher Susannah House." "Teacher Susannah," the little Quaker children called her, instead of "Miss House." She lived near by the Pennells, and as the school was at quite a distance she called every morning for the little boy, and took him with her. Every afternoon she brought him home, his hand in hers. One of his wretched memories of this school was the fifth day of each week, for on "fifth day" the boys were led two by two in a sober procession through the streets. The naughty boys of the "world's people" lined themselves up along the curb, taunted and called names at the little boys in their Quaker dress. "Quaker! Quaker!" they jeered, "How is thee?" which was certainly unkind and not sporting of them, for the Quakers had been very fair to people of other faiths and races, and had been, in the beginning, one of the first to tolerate other religions, as you know from your American history. The little Quaker children were teased also because they had to go to school on "Seventh Day" and twelve month, twenty-fifth. On this last day, all the "world's children" were having a gorgeous holiday, but the well-disciplined Quaker children continued on the even tenor of their quiet ways.

When Joseph was thirteen his father and mother moved away from the city to the suburb of Germantown. Joseph had never been very sturdy, and they felt that the country would be better for him than the city. Germantown in those days was almost country, and in a short walk, or run, one could get out into the real country. Joseph delighted in this change; he explored the woods, played Indian with the other boys, tramped along the creeks, and in winter skated and coasted to his heart's content. His health improved a great deal and he had completed his list of calamities and mishaps.

Although Joseph was a "regular boy" and, like all boys, had his "gang," he enjoyed tramping about quite alone, seeking beautiful things to draw. In and about Germantown were fine old gray stone houses that dated back to Revolutionary days. About them were great trees that shaded them, and the sun shining through their leaves made fascinating patterns on their walls. Although he had never been taught to draw, he seemed instinctively to know what would be beautiful on paper. Wherever he saw anything that delighted him, he sat right down, there and then, and drew it (he always had his pocket filled with pencils). This trait he had all his days, even if he were suddenly inspired to draw on a public street. In and about Germantown, he drew the lovely old houses and the old mills and bits of woodland and fields.

At just a little time before, boys who wanted to draw were apprenticed to learn a trade which required some skill in drawing. You recall, Winslow Homer, Abbey, and Saint Gaudens all were apprenticed. The custom was gradually dying out. The chances of Joseph Pennell's having an opportunity to learn to draw seemed slight at first. His parents gave to him the best education that they could— they sent him to the Germantown Friends' Select School.

In this school most of the children had wealthy parents, for the Quakers with their steady industry and thrift were seldom poor. However, Joseph's people were far less fortunate than most, and he was made unhappy by the contrast. He did not like the long hours spent each day in school, and was restless to be out, eager to be by himself, drawing. Nor did he like most of his teachers. His love of drawing at every opportunity displeased them mightily; they looked upon it as a foolish waste of time, besides, his using his left hand annoyed them very much. Among all his teachers there was only one he loved, and even she had no patience with his drawing. If she caught him drawing on a slate, she promptly washed it off, or, if his drawing was on paper, she would bend over him and write beneath it, "Satan finds some mischief still for idle hands to do."

Philadelphia was slowly awakening to an interest in art, and the Germantown Friends' Select School decided, as an experiment, to have a drawing-class. It was only in this class that Joseph was perfectly content and happy. The drawing-teacher was very much interested in his work and managed to inspire an interest in his students. At the beginning of one summer he offered a prize for the boy who brought back to him the best drawing from his vacation. One of the wealthy little Quaker boys had the good fortune that summer to have his parents take him all the way out to Yosemite Valley. Surely, he thought, with pride and satisfaction, no boy could find anything more beautiful, no child back in Germantown could find anything so wonderful to draw. Joseph Pennell stayed at home all that summer, and his choice for a drawing was an ugly old house across the street! When all the drawings were at last displayed and it came time to select the winner, Joseph's heart was heavy. His ugly old house—and Yosemite Valley! Joseph knew that there was beauty to be found in old ugly things, if seen through the eyes of an artist! Would his teacher know this? His teacher most happily did, and to the great surprise, almost shock, of the other boys, Joseph received the prize, a silver crayon-holder in a leather case. The boy who had drawn Yosemite, who had been cocksure, may have learned a lesson; it is hoped so. No true artist, no great artist, places himself before something beautiful and copies it, and thinks that such a copy will make a beautiful picture. A hideous old tramp, drawn with a beautiful line or painted with rich lovely color, is far greater art than a drawing of a beautiful woman crudely done.

However much Joseph and his teacher realized this, the other boys did not, and when he left school that day, shy, bewildered, and happy over his first prize, he was made miserable by the twitters and taunts of the other children. His old ugly house got a prize. What a joke! Any joy he may have had from that prize had flown; he was silent and wretched on his walk home.

Joseph Pennell was the first boy to graduate from this school, and in spite of his love of drawing in season and out, he managed to pass all his other subjects and graduate with honors. It was the year 1876—the year of the Centennial—which, as we have said, was held in Philadelphia. The boy chose as his graduation essay to write of the drawings that were shown at the art section of the Exposition. This was a good excuse for him to haunt the art rooms as much as possible. It was not the sculpture of John Quincy Adams Ward which fascinated him, but the drawings of Edwin Austin Abbey. To him Edwin Austin Abbey was a more important personage than even President Grant! The Centennial was an inspiration to him, as it was to all those in America who loved art. America was beginning to think seriously of an art of her own.

Pennell's school days were over, and they had not been happy years. In fact, he often said these six years were the most miserable of his life. What was he to do next? He had not the slightest doubt what he wanted to do, but how could it be managed? He wanted to be an artist, nothing else. His parents needed his help; he had to have money. His aunts, greataunts, and cousins most certainly felt that, now his school days were over, he should get to work and earn money. He knew that they would be shocked and horrified at his determination to be an artist. Quakers did not approve of "art" or art careers, any more than the Puritans had. They felt that trying to make themselves or their homes beautiful was "too worldly." Everything in their lives was very plain and austere. Neither in their dress nor in their homes did they permit any "ornaments" or "decorations." Nevertheless, without seeking "beauty," their homes were more beautiful than they realized. Their furniture was excellent; most of it came from England. It was made by two fine furniture-makers, Chippendale and Sheraton, and the plain simplicity of their rooms was lovelier than rooms cluttered with too much furniture and too many pictures. Joseph Pennell knew this simplicity was beautiful, even though his people never gave the matter a thought. But how was he going to make his family and his people consent that he become an artist? His father, although disapproving, never interfered, and did what he could to help his son. One of the tragedies of Pennell's life was the fact that his mother never approved! Her disapproval hurt him deeply, but it did not make him give up his ambition to be an artist.

The first summer after his graduation could not have been an altogether happy one for Pennell. His cousins and his aunts all thought he should be looking for a regular position. He was too old to be supported by his parents. Instead of seeking work that would have satisfied them, he drew all summer, up in his hot attic. He had by a very great piece of good luck made some money from his chickens, and with this money he bought plaster casts of hands and feet, pens, pencils, chalk, and books about artists. His father had always given to the boy what he could afford, but the boy's ambition had been stirred to greater effort by those weeks spent in the art section of the Centennial! Although he was working with all his heart and energy, he knew that his people felt that he was not doing the right thing. Some day he felt that he would prove to them that this time spent in a hot attic, drawing, was very much worth while; some day he knew he could give his parents money from his drawing.

At the end of the summer he took all of his work to the

Pennsylvania Academy School. He longed to be admitted to this art school. It was the best to be had in the city at that time, and free! He waited and waited for the decision about his drawings, waited to be sent for and told that he had been admitted. Instead, after many weary months he was sent for and asked to come and get his drawings. He had been rejected. One can feel his shame and humiliation when he brought those drawings home! One can almost hear an aunt say, "Thee has wasted thy time long enough; thy parents have been good and patient. Is it not time that thee earn money for them?" He knew that he could no longer put off working for a living at something far from his heart. He at last found himself a clerk in the Philadelphia and Reading Coal and Iron Company's offices. For a few minutes he must have been overwhelmed by a feeling of black despair at the gloomy prospect. However, he was very conscientious, and he was determined to give his employers the best he possibly could. He felt he must be worth the seven dollars a week they paid him.

The Centennial had, as we have said several times, a great effect on art in this country. For one thing, it resulted in the opening of a new art school in Philadelphia—the Pennsylvania School of Industrial Art. Joseph Pennell took his rejected pen drawings to this new school, and they at once accepted him as a pupil. Of course, his lessons had to be at night, for he was still working in the day, at the coal office. An art student at night, a clerk in a coal office by day! He worked unceasingly, and even managed to do some drawing in the coal office at slack times, getting some of his fellow workers to pose for him.

From the very first, line drawing fascinated him. He knew just what he wanted to be, and that was an etcher. To change and transform a plain piece of white paper by, as few lines and as beautiful as possible, into a work of art, was his ambition. In later years he wrote a book about etching for etchers. In it he said, "The great etching, by a great etcher is a great work of art displayed on a small piece of paper, expressed with the fewest vital, indispensable lines." These lines are not made with a pen, pencil, or brush, but with a needle—an etcher's needle! And they are not first made on a paper or canvas, but on a copper plate! The copper plate is first covered with a thin coating of wax, which is called "the ground." Then the etcher takes his needle and draws right on this "grounded plate." After this, the plate is put into an acid, which has no effect on the wax, but "burns," or "bites," as the etcher calls it, into the lines he has drawn. The line is then "bitten" into the copper plate. From this plate he prints his drawing on white paper. A good etcher always has his own press and does his own printing.

The beauty of an etching is in the beauty of the lines which the artist uses. He is not depending on paint and color; he must make his work a thing of beauty in black and white. How much he can show us with his line! First, of course, he shows the outline or form of what he is drawing. He does not use the same kind of line for the soft silky whiskers of an old man as he would for the side of a prison wall, nor the same line for a flying cloud that he would for a marble doorstep, nor yet the same line for a delicate lace ruffle that he would for the folds of a stiff satin dress! Shadows will fall across his pictures; these, too, he must show with his line.

Pennell said that all great etchers worked directly on their copper plate, that they did not make sketches on paper and then copy from them. Of course, when they printed from their drawing, the drawing was reversed, as though it were held before a mirror. This fact did not make the slightest difference to the real etcher, because the lines were as lovely and beautiful on one side of the paper as on the other. An etcher makes many prints from one plate, but after the plate becomes worn, then he destroys it.

Joseph Pennell, as perhaps you remember, wrote a book about Whistler. Although he was himself a famous etcher, he always considered the etchings of Whistler were better than his own. The greatest of all etchers was the Dutch artist, Rembrandt. Rembrandt and Whistler were both master painters and are more generally known for their paintings, but, nevertheless, what etchings they did were great indeed. Pennell considered Rembrandt's etching of his mother the finest etching in the world!

In Pennell's book on etching is a list of materials needed for one etching. This book is wider and longer than most books, and the pages are big, but this list of materials takes up three and a half pages! Three and a half big pages, for there are required for one etching a copper plate, celluloid films, needle points, etching ground, nitric acid, hydrochloric acid, turpentine, alcohol, kerosene, scrapers, etching rollers, ten yards of soft white muslin, canvas, and so on and on and on! Beautiful and simple as an etching may be when it is finished, the making of it so is not simple!

Pennell's first drawing on a copper plate was done when he was a student at the Academy of Industrial Art in Philadelphia. It was an old mill near Wister's Lane, but, unfortunately, no print of it remains for us today! His first sale came also when he was a student, for which he received one dollar!

Some of the teachers at this school were an inspiration to him, and others were not! He was, even as a student, very outspoken, and he expressed himself in no uncertain terms about some of the teaching done at this school; he stayed away from classes he did not approve of, and soon other pupils followed his example. He received a very polite, quiet note from the secretary, telling him that his name was no longer on the list of students. Nice and polite as it may have been, it meant that he was expelled. One of his friends went to the officials of the Academy—the Academy which had rejected his drawings done in that hot attic one summer—and asked them to look again at his etchings. This time he was accepted. His art had now come to mean more than anything on earth to him—nothing else mattered—and he gave up his position in the coal office and decided to settle down to grim hard work on his etchings.

It is easy to imagine the dismay and even horror and heartbreak that this step meant to his people! The matter was brought up before a Quaker meeting. What would they do with a Quaker who was so determined to pursue so worldly a career as art? After much discussion it was decided not to expel him from the Germantown meeting. It was remembered that there *had been* Quakers before him who had been artists; in fact, the "dean of American artists," Sir Benjamin West (who had helped Gilbert Stuart), had been a Quaker. Howard Pyle, a noted American illustrator who was prospering as an artist, was also a Quaker. No, Joseph Pennell was not dismissed from the Quaker meeting, but was a member in good standing of the Germantown meeting until the day of his death.

Pennell continued at the Academy until his orders came so fast that he had no time to do anything else but fill them. In 1880 (he was then twenty-three) he left the Academy and took a studio on Chestnut Street in Philadelphia. This studio he shared with another American artist who was to become well known—Harry Poore. Near their studio was the studio of a woman artist—Cecelia Beaux, who was also to become famous.

Joseph Pennell did not have the long, bitter struggle for success that so many artists must have; he never knew what it was to face starvation or want. It was his good fortune that people were becoming very much interested in etching, and so he found himself doing what was popular and in demand. He didn't exactly wake up one bright and shining morning to find himself famous, a prominent etcher, but he came very near it! In a very short time after what his family had considered a reckless jump—that is, giving up a good clerkship for what they felt to be a doubtful future

—he was earning an excellent living. He became one of the regular illustrators of *Scribner's Magazine* (he worked for this magazine for thirty years). The first set of finished drawings he did for the magazine were paid for on the spot. He was walking on air when he left their office, for the banknotes in his pocket made him feel like a newly-made millionaire. He was eager to get back to his home at Fisher's Lane, Germantown—eager to startle his family with all this wealth. His feet had wings as he tore up the familiar streets, and he burst into his house like a whirlwind. His delicate mother was upstairs in bed, and as the wings were still on his feet, he flew up the steps! From his pockets he brought his precious roll of banknotes. Now he was no longer in a hurry, for slowly, deliberately he laid one banknote after another upon her coverlet. He felt that he had proved to her—to them all—his aunts, cousins, greataunts —that he had not done a mad, selfish, foolish thing in leaving that coal office. This would prove to her that some day he could do far more for her—for them—than he would have been able to do had he continued at something for which he had no heart.

The year 1880 was an eventful one for Pennell, for, besides seeing his life's work well started, he met for the first time one who was to be his partner in this life work— Elizabeth Robbins. His marriage with Elizabeth Robbins was one of the most beautiful things of his life, and their marriage was one of the most perfectly happy and ideal that one might read of in story or history. Their tastes were in perfect harmony, for she was a writer and he was an artist;

WOOLWORTH BUILDING *by* Joseph Pennell

she wrote stories for his illustrations, and he made illustrations for her stories. They were married four years after their first meeting—a meeting which came about because Miss Robbins wanted Pennell to illustrate a story she was writing for *Scribner's*. They had both hoped to have their honeymoon in a gypsy caravan, but, unfortunately, this romantic plan had to be given up and their journey was made in an ordinary train. However, they had many, many years of wandering about wherever their fancy took them, in all parts of the world, in the happy, carefree fashion of the gypsies. Many of these wanderings were on a tricycle, for bicycles and tricycles were then all the rage. They tricycled all over Italy, seeking beautiful things to write about, beautiful things to illustrate. Together they explored France, Spain, Germany, Belgium, England, Wales, and Scotland—always in that endless quest of beauty! Wherever Pennell found anything that inspired him, lured his fancy, he sat himself down and drew it (as we may have said before), even if it were on a crowded thoroughfare. Perhaps it might be a beautiful cathedral—for he loved to draw the magnificent cathedrals of the Middle Ages—or perhaps it might be a quaint marketplace, or the narrow picturesque streets of an ancient town, but whatever it was that caught his fancy he drew it immediately. Once, when he was drawing on a street in England, a street thronged with people, a man stood at his shoulder for a long time, watching him. At last the man asked him what he was doing. "Minding my own business," Pennell answered. "Isn't it about time you were doing the same thing?"

Pennell became recognized both here and abroad as the foremost etcher of his day; his work was everywhere in demand, his opinion on etching was considered of utmost importance. Toward the end of his life he held many positions of eminence. He represented, for one thing, the American Academy of Arts in Belgium, and later on was made a member of the Royal Antwerp Academy.

The first book that Pennell and his wife did together was called *A Canterbury Pilgrimage*. Pennell was the favorite illustrator of many of the most famous and prominent writers both here and in England. Among his most beautiful books of etchings was one of *The Tuscan Cities,* which he illustrated for William Dean Howells. One of his last books was *Philadelphia—Old and New.*

After many years abroad, wandering all over Europe, Pennell and his wife returned to America to live. During the World War Pennell made many drawings of the war work done in England, France, and Belgium. As he said of this work, "Not only have I seen the wonder of work done in these three lands today, but before the war I saw it in Germany and Italy, and I am not going to make comparisons; but the Wonder of Work is more wonderful in the United States than anywhere else in the world today." After the war, the American Federation of Arts exhibited in the National Gallery of Art in Washington, D. C., fifty-one etchings and lithographs of Pennell, showing the war work done in America. Woodrow Wilson wrote him a letter of praise for this remarkable display.

There were a few things in America—the America that

Pennell loved—which were not to his liking, and with his way of saying exactly what he thought, he made his disapproval known. For one thing, he bitterly disapproved the hideous signboards that were stuck up all over our beautiful countryside, and he waged war against them.

Pennell and his wife went to live in Brooklyn, at the Hotel Margaret. From this hotel and from his broad windows he could revel in a sight that filled his soul with delight and ecstasy—the almost unbelievable beauty of New York City. And that is what he called New York City— "the Unbelievable City." It was the city among all in the world that inspired, enthralled him the most; it was the city he loved. During his last years he could hardly tear himself away from his window at the Hotel Margaret, for fear that some magic might turn that city into something more beautiful, glorious, glamorous than he had yet seen. The sky-scrapers in the early morning mist appeared like the shadowy towers of a fairy dream; in the twilight against the brilliant sapphire blue of the sky, with their lights blazing, twinkling like jewels studded against their sides, they made it an enchanted city from out *Arabian Nights!* The beauty of the scene held him spellbound; so breathlessly he drank in the beauty and splendor of it, that he often forgot to eat. Meals must wait. The magic before him was too fleeting; he must revel in its witchery while it was before him.

Pennell's last illness was swift, unexpected. As he lay in bed, dangerously ill with influenza, he begged his doctors to have his bed moved and brought beside his beloved

165

window, so that, perhaps for the last time, he might look upon his "Unbelievable City." It was a bitter disappointment that they dared not move him, but he accepted his disappointment with a sweet patience.

In his last illness he spoke of Whistler and the struggle that they had shared together, for to the last Pennell was a warm and loyal friend to the great painter. He himself was now content to die. His life had been a long one, thronged with vivid experiences. It had been so much worth while! He had made his will. Everything he had, his entire fortune of over a quarter of a million, was to be left to his country. America had been kind to him, had given him a start, and now she was helping and inspiring many other young artists to greater heights. That the future would see a great art here in America was a cherished hope! America had made a splendid beginning for so young a country. In the years to come, what wonderful things she might do!

"It's a beautiful life—it's a beautiful life," he repeated. And this beautiful life ended for him in a beautiful dream on April 23, 1926.

IX

JOHN SINGER SARGENT

America's Greatest Portrait Painter

MERICA'S FIRST GREAT PORTRAIT PAINTER, GILBERT STUART, WAS BORN ON DECEMBER 3, 1755, AND HER GREATEST PORTRAIT PAINTER, JOHN SINGER SARgent, was born January 12, 1856. So, but for a few weeks, a whole century lay between them. A hundred years is a long, long time for a beautiful princess to lie sleeping in a castle, but it is a very short time in the life of a country. Nothing, or no one, stirred within the Sleeping Beauty's castle walls, there was no sound to break the silence in all that one hundred years, unless perhaps one of the guards snored in his sleep! But those one hundred years that lay between these great artists were filled with movement, sound, and strife; everybody and everything was struggling, changing, and marching onward. These one hundred years seem far too short for all that was accomplished—as far too short as the other one hundred years seem far too long for idle sleeping.

America at the end of an extraordinarily busy century was still forging ahead, still growing. Proud as she had reason to be of her brief and eventful past, she was more concerned with the future. She was like a young person who lives each day fully and vividly, but is more eager and hopeful of the future and what it will bring. America felt that, no matter how much she had done, there was still greater and bigger things for her to do! And so, it was that what art she had accomplished, although not as a whole great as that of older nations, was fine enough to make her feel that some day she might rival them! All of the artists born within this hundred years were a promise of greater artists to come.

Gilbert Stuart was born in a bare little town in Colonial New England; John Singer Sargent was born in the beautiful Italian city of Florence. The Florence that he knew as a boy was little changed from what it had been at the very height of its great glory and power, four hundred years before. The fifteenth century was one of the most marvelous centuries in the whole history of art, and Florence led the world in her passionate love of art. Everyone within her city walls was a lover of the beautiful—her rich merchants, powerful nobles, priests, and citizens. When one of her great artists had finished a masterpiece, the whole city rejoiced and declared a holiday. The entire population turned out to honor him and do homage to his genius. Flowers were strewn along the way, music filled the air, a long procession of priests and citizens in gay holiday dress marched through the city streets to inspect the new creation of beauty. Old men, old women, young men and young women, boys and girls and little children, all came trooping. The city went wild with joy and pride.

John Singer Sargent

Along the thoroughfares and in the public squares of Florence were the statues of the world's supreme sculptors —Michelangelo, Donatello, and Verrocchio (sculptors without a rival save the ancient Greeks). The bronze doors of the Baptistry at Florence, Michelangelo had once declared "were so beautiful that they might fittingly be called the gates of Paradise." On the walls of the churches and monasteries were magnificent mural paintings. With a whole population so wrapped up, heart and soul, in art, is it any wonder that it was a beautiful city and that on every hand we see great masterpieces of architecture, sculpture, and painting?

Never was an American artist of whom it might be more truthfully said that he was born with a silver spoon in his mouth, than John Singer Sargent. His parents were not poor; they were wealthy. They did not distrust art, or disapprove of it; they loved and respected it. Moreover, Sargent as a child had all about him some of the world's most precious and marvelous art treasures! Sometimes, however, in this world, it is more surprising to find a man greatly successful who has had everything given to him, than one who has had to fight and struggle for victory. Sargent was not spoiled by having everything so beautifully done to make his way easy, for all his life he was a conscientious and hard worker.

It may seem surprising that John Singer Sargent is called an American artist at all! He was born in Italy, of American parents, but he lived his entire life abroad, only coming to America for visits, and he finally died in England. But in spite of this, Sargent stoutly insisted upon calling himself an American. He was very proud of his American citizenship. Once, in later years, when the King of England wished to knight him for his distinguished work, he politely but firmly refused to accept the honor, because it was not an honor that an American could accept. His disposition and character were too thoroughly American for him to ever consider becoming the citizen of another country.

Although Sargent was born abroad, and his entire life was spent there, his ancestry was wholly American. The Sargents had first come to America from England with that little band of Puritans under John Winthrop in 1630. They had from the first distinguished themselves in the early Colonial history, and today "the Sargent house," at Gloucester, Massachusetts, is a public shrine to this remarkable family. They had been prominent lawyers, doctors, clergymen, and writers. During the American Revolution they had served their country as valiant soldiers. One of them had written a popular song, "Life on the Ocean Wave." The inhabitants of Gloucester had been seafaring for generations; they were mariners and fishermen, so it is not surprising to read that many of the Sargent family were captains in the merchant service. This love of the sea had been passed on to Fitz William Sargent, the father of the great artist, and he had hoped that his son might some day enter the United States navy. So this all shows us that the Sargents of Gloucester were loyal and distinguished Americans.

John Singer Sargent's mother, the beautiful and talented Mary Newbold Singer of Philadelphia, came from an

American family as loyal and distinguished as the Sargents. Her family had first come to America from England in 1730. The Singers had always been a family of considerable wealth, and Mary Newbold Singer was an heiress in her own name. As a young girl she had traveled all over Europe, but it was the beauty of Italy that enchanted her more than the other countries, that cast a spell over her. She promised herself, when she left it, that some day she would return and make it her home. Her independent fortune and her love of Italy were to make a great difference in her life, the life of her husband and children. When she married Fitz William Sargent, he was a very prosperous and successful doctor, with a large practice in Philadelphia. Not only had he made a success with his practice, but he had written many books on surgery—books which he also illustrated. These books were used in most of the medical schools in the country. Four years after their marriage, Mrs. Sargent begged her husband to give up his work as a doctor and go to Italy to live. Her fortune, with the money he had already made, was enough for them to live on abroad; he need not continue with his practice. Mrs. Sargent had her way. Perhaps that is why she was always so gay, so light-hearted, and loved life so much, while her husband, who was not so enthusiastic about leaving America, was a silent man, somewhat stern and austere. The life his wife loved so devotedly was not the life he himself would have chosen. Giving up his practice, saying good-by forever to his patients, must have touched him deeply. But because he was made of the stern stuff of the Puritan, he made no complaint, but accepted grimly the fate allotted to him. Probably in those long, long years abroad he longed for his own work and his native land. His wife was radiantly happy, he told himself, and that must be his reward for the sacrifice.

The first home of the Sargents abroad, of course, was in Italy, and in that immortal city of Florence. It was here that their first son, John, was born on January 12, 1856, in a quaint old house near the River Arno. Mrs. Sargent was never content to stay long in one place. She moved eagerly and restlessly from one city, one country, to another. A year after John was born, a baby girl, Emily, arrived in Rome; the frail, delicate little Mary was born a few years later in Nice. The Sargents moved constantly, wandering all over Italy, Switzerland, France, Spain, Germany, and England. Between each new country there was always a return to Italy, for a visit. John Sargent spent his boyhood on trains and in hotels. He had very little opportunity for regular schooling, so he had private tutors. However, he could learn his history and geography the best way possible— that is, first hand and not out of books. He knew where all the cities of Europe were, not by locating them on a map, but by actually traveling to them. He knew where kings were born, where artists lived, and actually stood before many such an historic spot. One does not forget a lesson learned in so entrancing a fashion. Alas! it is too bad that a whole classroom of children, when asked to locate, say, Munich, Nice, or Biarritz, cannot just get on a train and go and find it, instead of standing before a big map and fumbling all over it with a pointer!

The Sargent children, in spite of their constant travel, made some very good friends—friends which they kept until they were grown up. These children, too, were like themselves—little travelers. Two of them were the sons of an American admiral (probably Dr. Sargent hoped they might interest John in the navy), another was a little girl named Violet Paget, who grew up to be a writer and used the name "Vernon Lee." It was a little boy of Spanish descent—a Benjamin Del Castillo—who was John's favorite "pal" for many years. These two little fellows, only nine, found their paths often in opposite directions, so they had to content themselves with long letters describing their new experiences. In this way they added to their own knowledge of places they themselves had seen. John wrote Ben a very interesting letter from Pau, a city in southern France, where the Sargents had gone for poor little Mary's health. John was nine at this time, and the letter, besides giving a vivid idea of what interested him, speaks of his drawing. Here is part of the letter:

Pau,
April 16, 1865

Dear Ben:

We got to Pau on Wednesday. We stayed at Toulouse a day, and Mamma took Emily and me to the Museum, we saw the pole and wheels of a Roman chariot and many pictures and statues. The next day we got to Bordeau, in the afternoon Mamma took Emily and me to the Cathedral where King Richard II of England was married to an Austrian Princess. The windows of the Cathedral were filled with beautiful stained glass; one of the windows was round, and the glass was of a great many colors. The Cathedral is very old. Bordeau is a fine old city. The quay on which our hotel was is very wide, and the river has a great lot of large ships on it and a great many steamers. We left so early the next morning that I had not time to draw any of them, but they would have been too difficult for me, I think. . . . We came from Bordeau to Pau by rail-way in about five hours. We had a very cold room in the hotel and the weather was very bad for a while; it snowed every day for about a week, and sometimes it snowed hard, but the snow melted directly. After that, the weather cleared up and we had some very fine days, so Mary could go out in the carriage. We heard a cuckoo whistle so prettily. We see the mountains covered with snow from our windows, they look so beautiful. Poor little Mary is getting thinner every day. She does not care for anything any more. Emily and I bought her some beautiful Easter eggs, but she would not look at them. She never talks nor smiles now. Goodbye, dear Ben, write soon.

Yours affectionately,
John S. Sargent.

There! We learn from this letter many interesting things about this little nine-year-old boy and the life he led. We know that the family journeys were not all pleasure and joy, for sometimes they came to hotels that were cold and uncomfortable, probably bleak and most unhomelike. Then, too, we learn that John was a very tender, warm-hearted, devoted little brother to his sick baby sister. It is easy to imagine, from this letter, how deeply it touched him that "she never talks nor smiles now." He had certainly hoped, with all his boyish heart, that she would be at least impressed by the sight of "some beautiful Easter eggs." One can easily picture his bitter disappointment, bewilderment, almost alarm, as the baby failed to be in the least impressed by this gift of gifts at Easter time! Surely he thought something must be sadly wrong with his little sister. This side of John Singer Sargent, this warm, loving, tender side, some people in after years failed to recognize. There were those who thought him "cold" and indifferent. Throughout his days he was always the same devoted, loving brother.

The most important sentence in this letter—as far as his future fame was concerned—was: "the river has a great lot of large ships on it and a great many steamers. We left so early the next morning that I had not time to draw any of them." It is a large ambition for a boy of nine to even *think* of drawing ships!

John's mother was always painting. Her water-color box was open before her, wherever they went. It was her paints that John used first. A month after this letter from Pau the Sargents were again on the wing, and John wrote another letter to Ben Del Castillo. This letter was from Biarritz, a resort on the Bay of Biscay. In this letter John again refers to ships and drawing. It begins:

Biarritz,
May 18th, 1865.

Dear Ben:

Day before yesterday we went to San Sebastian where there is a fort on the top of a hill. Near the foot there are a great many English graves; I have a little picture of one in my album. I also made a little picture of the Battery and a good many ships.

The boy's father most likely secretly hoped that this interest in drawing ships would lead to a greater interest in the ships themselves, rather than the drawing of them. It was still Dr. Sargent's hope that his son might some day enter the United States navy. Mrs. Sargent, because of her own love of painting, encouraged her boy to continue his drawing. John was as yet far too young to make a definite decision about his future.

Dr. Sargent had left his family at Biarritz and had gone on a visit to America. After a few months, the family went to London to meet him on his return. John had never been in London before, and he was very much impressed by it. But his visit was far too short, far too crowded with sight-seeing, for him to have time to write to his good friend "Ben"; the letter had to wait until they got to Paris. From Paris he wrote to Ben of the wonders of London:

Paris,
Oct. 13, 1865.

Dear Ben:

I am sorry that you did not get the letters that we wrote you last. We have often thought of writing to you since we knew that you had not received them, but we were so busy sight-seeing that we have not had time. We spent several weeks in London and the things which interested me most were the Zoological Gardens, the Crystal Palace, the South Kensington Museum. At the Zoological Gardens, we saw the lions fed. I rode on a camel's neck and Emily and I rode on an elephant. At the Crystal Palace, we saw models of some animals which were upon earth before man. I copied several of them. At the South Kensington Museum, we saw some very fine paintings of Landseer's, the animal painter, and a very fine picture by Rosa Bonheur, called the "Horse Fair."

So you see John, although not ten, drew wherever he went. At this early age he had seen many wonderful things and a great many marvelous paintings and works of art. His mother always took her children to the art museums of every large city that they visited. Mrs. Sargent was a very wise mother—she wanted her children to be strong and healthy. John was, all the days of his life. She did not force them to hours of long and hard study. She believed that they would remember more vividly the things they had actually seen, than if they had only read about them from books! Today, boys and girls may go to the movies, or have them in their schools, showing all the strange and wonderful places in the world. Travel pictures and nature pictures make study ever so much more interesting. The Sargent children did not have travel pictures to go to, as there were no movies, but instead, their lives were the "movies" themselves, for new scenes flitted before their eyes almost as rapidly as the films of a movie! After the Sargent children had seen anything very interesting or historic, they went to books to learn more about it.

When John was twelve the Sargent family went to Spain for the summer. On their way to Gibraltar in a boat they were caught in a terrible storm and their ship was in great peril of going to the bottom of the sea. John was very calm, although he knew of the peril they were in and saw the fear of the other passengers. Throughout his life he was always calm in the face of danger. Summer was not the time to visit Spain, for the heat was fearful and most of the hotels they came to were wretched. In spite of this miserable combination of intense heat and terrible hotels, the family managed to get to the art galleries of Spain. Here, for the first time, John saw the paintings of the great Spanish artist and portrait painter, Velasquez, whose work was to make a very important impression upon him in later years, for he admired Velasquez very much.

When John Singer Sargent was thirteen it was decided that he was to be an artist. His mother, of course, had longed and hoped for this decision. She had cherished a drawing of his made when he was only four, and in the years between had encouraged him to draw wherever he went, gladly sharing with him her own paint box. Dr. Sargent very likely was disappointed. He had so hoped for a splendid career in the United States navy. However, he was made of the stuff of the real Puritan—what God had ordained must be accepted. God, it seemed, had given his son a talent that must not be hurled away, or buried as the man in the Bible did with his "talent." It was God's will that his son should be an artist, and God's will be done! Dr. Sargent put away all thought of his son's entering the navy. His son must take his career seriously and give to it all he had in him. The boy now began to work in earnest, drawing hard each day. He asked for criticism. He wanted his work just right. But it was a little too correct at first; he was too careful of details. These first drawings were very little more artistic than his father's drawing had been in the medical books. Dr. Sargent might have drawn a very perfect, very exact picture of a pair of lungs, the inside of the ear, or the digestive tract, but perfect as they might have been, they were not works of art. John Sargent drew his flowers and his scenes with the same accuracy as his father had hearts and livers. He would have to learn to draw more freely and leave more details out of his pictures. He had, as his first teacher said, "much to unlearn."

When he was fourteen he entered the Academia della Belle Arti (Academy of Fine Arts) at Florence, Italy. After his first year at the Academy he won the annual prize which was given. When vacation time came he and his mother worked very hard together, sketching everything that they could. Mrs. Sargent was determined that her husband's wish in this should be carried out—that the art career must be taken seriously if it was to be taken at all. Dr. Sargent, since he had given up all hope of a naval career, must be convinced that it was for the best. Mrs. Sargent did not praise her son much, even though she encouraged him.

At fourteen John Singer Sargent was a tall, slim, charming boy with delightful, frank manners. He was a very healthy and strong boy, so he walked with a firm stride, carrying himself well. His hair was dark, his eyes bright blue, his skin clear and fresh. Although he seemed shy and reserved, he could very easily be made to laugh, and on rare occasions could show a hot temper. Besides his passion for drawing, he was always very fond of music, and when he was young took much joy from his mandolin. You recall that as a man he entertained the family of Edwin Austin Abbey at their home in England, by his playing on the piano for them in the evenings?

179

There was a very grave family decision to be made when John Singer Sargent was eighteen. Where was he to be sent to finish his art training—Paris or London? Paris in those days was considered a very gay, wicked city, with far too many temptations for a young man. It was a serious matter to decide. The better teachers, they felt, were to be had in Paris. Dr. Sargent, although a Puritan at heart and opposed to worldly, frivolous things, was a wise and sensible man, and he fully appreciated the fact that Paris was a better city for the young artist to learn art than London. He trusted his son (as he had every reason to) and so it was he himself who took the boy one day to the studio, in the Latin Quarter, of Carolus Duran, who was the best teacher and the most popular portrait painter in Paris. John Sargent, with his drawings under his arm, stood, shy and embarrassed, beside his somewhat stern father, whose hair was now gray, but who still held himself stiff and erect like the Puritans of old. Carolus Duran looked over these drawings which were so very, very carefully done—drawings filled with too many little details. It was Carolus Duran who had said that John Sargent had "much to unlearn," but he added that he also saw signs of promise far above the average. John Sargent was promptly accepted by the well-known artist as a pupil. In a short time he became Carolus Duran's most promising and favorite pupil. Sargent was a hard worker, thorough, careful, and conscientious. Above all, he was modest, for he felt that his work could be improved, and he constantly struggled to make it so. His teacher, Carolus Duran, was a handsome fellow of Spanish descent, who had had a long and bitter struggle to win his success. This struggle he could not easily forget, and when his favorite pupil, later on, began to get success without cruel and black hours, Carolus Duran became very jealous of him. At first, however, the pupil and teacher were on the best of terms. Duran was an ardent admirer of the great Spanish portrait painter, Velasquez (the painter whose work Sargent had seen that hot summer in Spain). Duran preached "Velasquez"—"Velasquez" in season and out to his students; he told them to study his work and to make copies of his paintings which hung in the Louvre. Sargent very naturally came to admire Velasquez very much. After he had decided to be a portrait painter he made a trip to Holland, to study the work of two other very great portrait painters, Rembrandt and Frans Hals. In Germany he studied Holbein—another of the world's masters of portraiture.

Although Sargent had not the bitter struggle for success that Carolus Duran had had, few young men would have given up all pleasures to work the long grinding hours that he did while studying in the Latin Quarter. He knew that there is no royal road to fame and that he would never succeed without hard work. He got up every morning at seven so that he might reach the studio by eight. His working hours were from eight in the morning until ten at night, with just one hour for his dinner. Once he became an art student, he ceased to be a traveler; in fact, he was rarely, if ever, seen outside the Quarter! The Latin Quarter in those days was vivid and picturesque; the artists jauntily wore a costume all their own—tam-o'-shanters perched cockily on their heads, brilliant sashes about their waists, flowing ties, big wide velvet trousers which were caught in tight at the ankles. John Sargent quietly spurned all this, and, instead, dressed with fastidious care and in the best of taste, for Sargent, all his life, was in appearance the spick-and-span man of the world.

Although Sargent had money and Saint Gaudens had had none, both artists were far too absorbed in their work to join in the gay life of the Quarter. Both men took their work too seriously to bother with the frivolous, devil-may-care side of the Latin Quarter. Sargent was human and once in a while he did join their festivities. The maddest, wildest festival of the year was that of *mi-Carême,* and probably there was nothing left for him but to take part in it. In a letter to Ben Castillo (the two friends were still corresponding), he described this festival of festivals in the Latin Quarter. "Dancing, toasts and songs," he wrote, "lasted until four. In short, they say it was a very good example of a Quartier Latin ball. The whole Quarter was out all night in the wildest festivity, quite surpassing anything I have ever seen in the Italian festival. I enjoyed our spree enormously."

After two years of very hard work in the studio of Carolus Duran, Sargent left the Latin Quarter to make a long trip—the longest and most unusual of his life. At twenty he was going to see, for the first time, his native land! How would it impress him? He was a European in everything except his citizenship; he was steeped in the culture of the Old World; he spoke several languages as fluently as English; he knew the history and literature of Europe, and the art of ancient, mediæval, and modern times, to his finger tips. Would he be disappointed in America? It was the year of the Centennial in Philadelphia, the Centennial which was so important and encouraging to American artists. How would he think the work exhibited compared with that of the great art galleries of the world? Sargent was always reserved. We cannot quote him as saying this or that. He was never a good speaker. But one thing was very evident—that something in America held him and touched some answering chord! He was among his own countrymen. This was his own, his native land! He knew that no matter where he might roam, no matter what ancient splendor he might see, America was his country. He might transplant himself and his art, but the roots would remain deep and firm in his native soil.

Sargent was only twenty when his painting was exhibited at the Salon in Paris. When he was barely twenty-two his portrait of his teacher, Carolus Duran, was exhibited at the Salon, and besides receiving "honorable mention," it received considerable attention and praise! This was remarkable for one so young, and a "foreigner," for, although Sargent had always lived abroad, he was considered in Paris as an "American." Only a few years later, when he was twenty-six, all Paris hailed him as the most successful painter of the year and the rival of her own very popular artists. That year he had two most-talked-of and conspicuous portraits at the Salon. He now had as many commissions for portraits as he could possibly accept—portraits for which he received very high prices.

Year after year, Sargent's portraits were much praised. He had very little criticism at first; his success was a steady one. However, the seventh year that Sargent exhibited was an exception. He presented a portrait that was not greeted with praise, but with furious and violent criticism and dissension. In fact, the portrait created a scandal and threw Paris into an uproar. This portrait, called Madame X, now hangs in the Metropolitan Art Museum in New York City. It is a painting of a Madame Gautreau, a Parisian beauty. Madame Gautreau was what was called a professional beauty, because she made her chief business and labor in life her beauty. She considered nothing more important than working and struggling to add to her beauty. When she saw Sargent's portrait of her exhibited, she was very indignant and wanted it taken down from the walls of the Salon. The portrait, she felt, showed too plainly that she was a shallow, vain woman, and a woman who thinks most of her beauty and clothes. All Paris took up the discussion and a violent storm broke over the portrait in art circles. All sorts of foolish, hateful, and idiotic things were said of Sargent. It was claimed that he took a wicked delight in bringing out on canvas, the mean, weak, or selfish traits of character that his sitters felt were well hidden deep in their souls. This is nothing but pure rubbish and nonsense, although it was repeated over and over many times in his life. After the uproar over the Gautreau portrait it was often claimed that Sargent had some strange black magic by which he could read people's souls! Sometimes people said they were afraid to have him paint them, for fear he "would show them up" in their worst light. This was very far from true. Sargent was too kindly a man to betray to the world any weakness or failing he might see in people who sat before him. Sargent painted what he saw before him, and perhaps his sitters sometimes quite plainly showed traits that they did not realize they had. Many of the criticisms of Sargent's work are very contradictory. Here, on one hand, we have those who charge him with looking too deeply into the souls of the people he painted, and on the other hand, there are those who say that he only painted what was on the surface and that he did not have the power to see behind the faces and dress of his sitters! Sargent took all this contradictory criticism somewhat like a stoic, for he was not puffed up by praise nor overwhelmed by fault-finding. He had too much good common sense to become vain and cocksure, or humiliated and depressed!

Shortly after the Gautreau painting, which has since been very highly praised, Sargent left Paris and went to England to make his home. He took a house at 31 Tite Street, which was the very house in Chelsea that had once been Whistler's! Whistler had painted the house a vivid yellow inside, which, as some one once said, gave one the impression of walking inside an egg! However, Sargent and Whistler were very different types of men, and Sargent's home was very different from Whistler's. Whistler had come to England twenty years before, and he had not been very popular. How would London feel toward another

American artist? Whistler had paved the way, and although he had not been at first cordially received, England had in time recognized his genius. Sargent was unknown in London, and it was Whistler himself who was the first to call attention to his young countryman. Whistler was very generous to the young portrait painter, for he wanted Sargent's way to be easier than his own had been. Sargent, in turn, was a great admirer of Whistler, for he once said that "Whistler's use of paint was so exquisite that if a piece of canvas were cut from one of his pictures, one would find that in itself it was a thing of beauty." Sargent and Whistler were friends until Whistler died.

Sargent was a success in London from the first. The English liked this cultured, fine-looking artist who had a fine reserve and dignity. The aristocracy of Great Britain came flocking to his studio to be painted. The list of people that he came to paint, both in England and America, is a long and imposing one. In America he painted the portraits of two Presidents, Theodore Roosevelt and Woodrow Wilson, and the presidents of several universities, besides a long list of notables in many walks of life—poets, actors and actresses, statesmen, and those socially prominent.

As success came to Sargent he changed little. He never sought society, but lived simply and quietly. He was always devoted to his family, and after his mother's death his tenderness and consideration to his aged father was very beautiful. Old Dr. Sargent liked to speak of "my son John," and there was in his voice a ring of deep pride and love as he spoke the words. John S. Sargent never married;

his sisters were his hostesses when he entertained. Perhaps because Sargent's life was without a "romance" that the newspapers could "write up," he was often accused of being cold and without feeling. But those who knew him best knew that this was unjust. He was a splendid and loyal friend, and the friendships which he made in childhood he kept through life, and none could have been a more devoted son or brother. There are many stories told of his generosity and kindness of heart, especially to artists less fortunate than himself. There was nothing he would not do for anyone in trouble; he would even stop anything he happened to be doing to make a sudden journey of mercy. Once an American artist fell ill and his wife had no one to turn to for help. Her husband had been earning their living teaching painting. Although almost unknown to Sargent, he not only came to their rescue with money, but he did more, he took the artist's classes and taught them until he was well enough to return to them himself. This kind of generosity is more beautiful than merely giving money. There is no end to the stories of Sargent's great tenderness and goodness. There are many many people who have good reason to know that he was not "cold."

There are numerous legends repeated of Sargent's experiences with his sitters, but they are only legends and most likely there is very little truth in them. For instance, there is a story of a woman who kept twisting her mouth into all sorts of ugly and ridiculous positions as Sargent tried to paint her. At last he is supposed to have suggested that "we leave it out altogether." Then there is another story of a woman who came to Sargent's studio and insisted upon being painted with a very gorgeous jewel crown upon her head! Of course, Sargent objected because she looked utterly ridiculous, as she had no right to wear any crown; but the woman insisted that she had bought the crown to be painted. Thereupon Sargent is said to have suggested that he make a separate painting of the bejeweled crown on a canvas of its own. These are only "stories" pure and simple. John S. Sargent was firm with sitters, but he was always courteous and he never deliberately tried to make them feel ridiculous.

One of the most interesting accounts—and a true one —of his sitters, was of the Spanish dancer, Carmencita. The portrait was painted in New York City, where Carmencita had "taken the town by storm." Everyone was marveling and raving about her dancing. Her beauty was as sensational as her dancing. Sargent was anxious to paint the portrait of this vivid creature, and she gave her consent. But he had no idea of what a task he had let himself in for. She was wild and untamed. Sometimes she wanted to romp while her portrait was being painted; at other times she would be in an ugly, sullen mood and would think nothing of hurling things about the studio or at some one! Sargent had to invent all sorts of ways to keep her amused and good-natured. He tried painting his nose a bright red! This delighted her, and she kept her eyes upon it until that, too, bored her. Then he pretended to swallow his cigar. All else failing, he bribed her with trinkets to keep still. This portrait of the Spanish dancer is one of Sargent's most celebrated paintings and now hangs in the Luxembourg Galleries in Paris. Carmencita is painted in an elaborate and rich silk dress of orange and black, and Sargent has managed to give us the impression that she is about to spring into the steps of one of her sensational dances. It is a dazzling picture and one that recalls to our minds that Sargent had admired the portraits of the great Spanish painter, Velasquez.

After one of Sargent's visits to America he had a very unusual, startling experience—an almost unheard-of experience of reading his own death notice! Probably many a great man has had the desire to have this opportunity, but he could never hope to have his desire fulfilled. A cablegram had been sent from London to America saying "John S. Sargent, the American artist, died here today after a short illness." Big glaring headlines greeted this report and some American newspapers wrote long editorials about John S. Sargent, his life and his work. But the report was not true, for John S. Sargent was very much alive at the time and was, in fact, reading with much interest the accounts of his death! It was another artist by the name of Sargent who had died. It must have been a very interesting experience to him to know just what was going to be said about him at his death.

Sargent became very tired of what he called his "society pictures." He said women did not actually say "Make me beautiful," but he knew they wanted him to, without their saying it. You perhaps remember Gilbert Stuart felt the same way, and it also annoyed him. On one occasion,

Sargent, who was at the time painting a mother and son together in a portrait, said, "I wish the darn thing were finished. The mother keeps getting younger and younger, while the boy keeps getting older and older!" It was a great source of joy and pleasure for him to be given the commission to work on the murals at the Boston Library. In doing this work he could please himself and not some vain and silly sitter. This work fascinated him, and few people realize that he worked on this gigantic task for thirty years.

Perhaps Sargent received more delight from painting the portraits of children than he did from some grown-ups. Children had at least no artificial poses and foolish notions of how they wanted to be painted. He could be sure they would be natural. Two of his greatest and most famous portraits are of children. One is of a little English girl— Hon. Laura Lister—and the other is of a little American girl—Beatrice Goelet. Both of these paintings have received high praise from the critics and are world favorites. The portrait of Beatrice Goelet is generally said to be one of the artist's masterpieces. Beatrice, as she is dressed in the portrait, is a quaint and picturesque little figure, with her long full skirt of striped gray and pink. Her pale golden hair is tied back with a pink ribbon. She stands sweetly, shyly, and appealingly before us, beside a large gilt cage in which a cockatoo is perched. She is so altogether charming and lovely, that it is small wonder the portrait is called a masterpiece. This portrait, and that of "Miss Alexander" by Whistler, will hold their own among the world's great paintings of children.

John Singer Sargent received high honors from many nations. Sometimes it has been said that a great man is not as appreciated in his own country as in others. But this cannot be said of Sargent, for America was warm and generous in her pride in him and he received much happiness from the honors she heaped upon him. Few artists in their lifetimes have had the praise and success that was John Sargent's. France made him a Chevalier of the Legion of Honor, and England a member of the Royal Academy. We have already spoken of the fact that the King of England offered him a knighthood. His answer to this honor is interesting:

"I deeply appreciate your willingness to propose my name for the high honor to which you refer and I hold it as one to which I have no right to aspire, as I am not one of His Majesty's subjects, but an American citizen."

On the afternoon of April 14, 1925, Princess Mary of England and her husband, Viscount Lascelles, came to John Singer Sargent's studio at 31 Tite Street, to pose for a portrait he was painting of them. They sat for a few hours and found the great artist as genial and as gracious as usual. This portrait was never finished, for that night John S. Sargent lay down, without any sign, to his eternal rest. The parlor maid who called him at his rising hour of eight received no answer to her knocking. When at last she entered the room, she found the great artist, as she said, "peaceful like a little child sleeping." It was the way he would have liked to die—to slip away from this world quietly and unrecognized.

Sargent's death created a tremendous sensation both here and abroad, and exceptional homage was paid to the dead artist. Memorial services were held in Westminster Abbey, which was a remarkable tribute to an artist and an American. During the services the flag hung at half mast from the Westminster Abbey tower. At the same time that these services were being held in England, a solemn requiem mass was being sung in the Church of St. John the Evangelist, in Boston. Beneath his portraits, which were in the public museums of many countries, memorial wreaths were hung.

John Singer Sargent, America's most distinguished portrait painter, was buried in England on the very day he had planned to set sail for America. And so fate decreed that he was to die, as he lived, away from his native soil, but with it in his mind and his heart!

X

THOMAS NAST

America's First Great Cartoonist

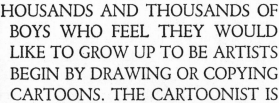HOUSANDS AND THOUSANDS OF BOYS WHO FEEL THEY WOULD LIKE TO GROW UP TO BE ARTISTS BEGIN BY DRAWING OR COPYING CARTOONS. THE CARTOONIST IS one "artist" who is admired and worshiped the country over by small boys. When a little fellow has made a good copy of a newspaper or magazine cartoon, he can be pretty certain that he will have an enthusiastic group of "pals" ready to shout in chorus, "Oh, say, but you're a *great* artist!" And in their voice may be a faint ring of envy—for they, too, would relish drawing a good cartoon. The young artist himself is fairly bristling with pride at his accomplishment. He is sure his friends are correct—that he is a "great artist." Although girls don't as often try to draw cartoons, they are quite as interested in them as their playmates among the boys. That is why the story of "cartooning" in America ought to be written.

Many great artists have been great cartoonists, but once in a while there have been great cartoonists who have not been great artists. This may sound very confusing and bewildering at first, but when you think it over it will be clear.

Of course, it is better that a cartoonist be an artist and that he have an excellent art training, but there have been cartoonists who have made a name for themselves without being "artists" and without much, if any, training.

Cartooning is one of the "graphic arts," which include printing and the illustrations in newspapers, books, and magazines. If you look the word "graphic" up in the dictionary, you will find the first meaning is "writing," the second, "illustrating ideas in pictures or diagrams." That is just what a cartoonist does—illustrates ideas by "pictures or diagrams." It is the "idea" which is very important, as important as an idea is in writing. Once in a while we find a cartoonist whose ideas are more clever, more interesting, more powerful than his drawings are fine. What a splendid combination it is when the drawings and ideas are equally strong and good! This combination is what makes a truly great cartoonist who is also a great artist! When the ideas are better than the drawings we might say the cartoonist is more like an author than an artist, for instead of writing his ideas he draws them.

A cartoonist, to most boys and girls, is the one who draws the pictures in the "funny sheets." But if they turn their newspapers over to the editorial page, they will find one cartoon which is not supposed to be "funny," especially before election time! These cartoons on the editorial pages, in a few strong lines, often tell us in a dramatic picture what is wrong—and sometimes right—with our politicians. They give us a vivid idea of our government—give it in a way that would take a writer columns to describe. The cause of peace and war has often been presented by a cartoonist in a manner so dramatic, so moving, so forceful, as to have more effect than a dozen lectures! Besides politics, cartoonists have often shown up the daily life of the people. Sometimes in a few strong lines they give us an idea of the foolish, mean, or selfish side of society, or showing, once in a while, something in society that is fine and inspiring. Most often cartoonists picture, in a powerful, dramatic way, something in society or in politics that needs reforming, and they do it in a bold and fearless manner and often very stern and grim. We shall speak again of the "funny sheets" with their daily continued story of a "family" or a boy or girl. These stories are not only "funny," but sometimes they are so real and true that we become very fond of the people in them and look forward to seeing them each day as we do our best friends.

One of the world's greatest cartoonists, and a great artist, was an Englishman named William Hogarth, who died in 1764, about ten years before the American Revolution. He has been called the "the father of English cartoonists." Hogarth was very much interested in the social life of the people of his times, for it was a period when many were coarse, vulgar and vain. He showed up in a brilliant and bold way the weakness and viciousness of this class of society. His cartoons had humor and wit. They made others laugh, but they also made them realize how stupid and coarse these people actually were! He made a remarkable series of what we call "society cartoons." Hogarth's drawings of the social life in England at the time in which he lived were works of art. He has his place among the great artists of the world. Whistler considered Hogarth one of the greatest of artists!

For the next fifty to sixty years cartooning began to flourish in Europe. There were splendid schools of cartooning in the leading countries abroad. But it was not until the beginning of the Civil War that America had a cartoonist who could rival those of Europe. America's first great cartoonist, and the "the father of cartoonists in America," was Thomas Nast.

America was Thomas Nast's country by adoption, and he served it well. He was born in the military barracks of the little fortified town of Landau in Germany in 1840. His father, a kindly, good-natured German, even though he was fearless in expressing his opinions, was a musician in the Ninth Regiment Bavarian Band. Thomas inherited from his father two traits—kindliness and fearlessness. However, his talent was not to be music, but art; his instrument was to be a pen, not a trombone!

Thomas, a nice roly-poly baby, was the pet and joy of his father's regiment, for babies were not a very usual experience in an army barracks. But this happy existence was to come to an end when Thomas was still a very little fellow. War clouds hung over Germany. As we have said, Thomas's father was fearless in expressing his opinion, and his opinions of his government were not what was expected of a German soldier. One day a friend and officer called him aside and gave him some wise advice. For his future peace and happiness he had better take himself out of the country. The officer suggested that he go to America, for in that country he would be permitted more freedom of speech than in the German army. The thought of America appealed to him; the officer's advice seemed to him very wise. He left Landau with his family. Later on he enlisted on an American vessel. While he was on the American boat, his family stayed for a while in France. It was decided at last that Mrs. Nast take her family and come to New York City. Thomas Nast was only six years old when, from the deck of the ocean liner, he had his first view of New York City. He was happy that he had come to America; his first impression of his new land lasted with him all his days.

The first home of the Nasts was on Greenwich Street. At that time the neighborhood and street were filled with quiet, respectable families. Little Thomas couldn't speak one word of English the first day that he was sent to the public school in the neighborhood of Greenwich Street. It is a hard experience for any little boy, hard and forlorn. He was most likely desperately homesick, for his companions at school tormented him almost beyond endurance. They took advantage of the fact that he could not speak the English language and played all sorts of tricks on him. He had to keep reminding himself how happy he had been that first day on the deck of the boat, and hoped that some day he would again be happy at the thought of America. Almost any new boy in any neighborhood is teased unmercifully for a while, until he makes his mark. It is one of the strange ways of boys the world over. The fact that he spoke another language and his first few words were spoken with a foreign accent, only filled the boys about him with a more wicked joy than with the usual "new boy."

Thomas was glad to get away from the neighborhood, even if their next house was said to be haunted. "Ghosts" at least would not tease him, and at twelve o'clock, when this ghost was said to be wandering about, Thomas was in a fine, heavy, peaceful sleep. At any rate, he never saw the "ghost," and he liked the new neighborhood and was very happy once again to be in America. Near by their new home Thomas discovered a store where they sold crayons to artists. The owner of the store gave to the delighted boy broken pieces of crayons he could not use. Thomas filled his pocket with them and went off jubilantly to his new school. In this school there were many children of German parentage, and the boy had friends with whom he could talk and was understood. He set to work at once to use his precious gift of crayons to draw pictures of his friends. One day he drew a picture of an African capturing a lion. His friends were excited and jubilant, quite ready to proclaim him "an artist." One of the older boys grabbed the drawing and dashed with it to the teacher. Thomas was afraid for a moment, for should he be drawing pictures in school? What would the teacher say? To his surprise and delight, the teacher did not scold him, but instead held the drawing up to the class for their admiration. It was Thomas Nast's first triumph as an artist, his first moment of victory in the New World!

From then on he drew everything, everywhere. His papers at school were covered with drawings, and so were the walls of his haunted house. He was certainly beginning to make a name for himself in this new neighborhood. The boys no longer teased him, but stood about admiring his skill. There was one bully who still dared to torment him—a boy far bigger than himself—and one day he turned upon him in fury and gave him a right royal beating. In fact, the bully had to be rescued from the outraged little Thomas! He was bold and fearless and he could draw; the other boys were now proud to say he was their friend.

One day Thomas came home from school to find his mother quite overcome with joy! The father of the family was to be once more with them! She sent Thomas flying to the bakery to get something especially wonderful for the great event. On his way home from the bakery a cab stopped near him at the curb and a big man flew out of it and grabbed the boy into his arms, crushing him, and the precious purchase from the bakery, to him in a bear-like hug. For a moment Thomas thought he was being kidnapped, or that a robber envied him his bundle! It was his father, his big, hearty, loving father, who had been so long separated from his family. What a reunion! The Nast family never forgot it. It was a day of days!

Like so many fathers, the elder Nast had an idea of just what he would like his son to be—an idea quite different from the son's own desire! The father wanted his boy to follow in his footsteps and be a musician. In fact, he was so insistent that Thomas did try being one for a while. But it was hopeless; the boy was an artist, and not a musician. His father at last gave in and sent his son to a drawing-class which was taught by a graduate from a German paint-ing academy. The teacher recognized at once that the boy had unusual talent, but, unfortunately, the lessons had to come to a sudden end, for a fire completely burned out this teacher's studio. After trying to practice drawing by himself for a while at home, a friend helped him get into the Acad-emy of Design. He was elected to the life class, which was considered the most difficult class, the one for advanced students. Visitors at the Academy were very much im-pressed by the work of the fat little German boy, and everyone felt that they were beholding an artist who would make a name for himself.

One day when he was about fifteen he was so encour-aged by the praise of those about him, that he put his drawings under his arm and went to call upon a Frank Leslie who had established a new magazine called *Frank Leslie's Weekly*. Thomas Nast made a cartoon afterward of their interview, in which he showed the tall editor look-ing down upon a small boy who was almost as broad as he was long! Leslie examined the drawings that the boy had with him and found them very good. But to the editor the artist was far too young to be taken seriously. As it happens so often in fairy tales, the boy was given a task to do which seemed impossible—a task given with the idea and hope that it was impossible.

"Very well," said Mr. Leslie. "Go down to Christopher Street next Sunday morning when the people are boarding the ferry, and make a picture of the crowds just as the last call of 'All aboard' is shouted. Do you understand?" Mr. Leslie expected the boy to be frightened and overcome by such a request. Surely a boy of fifteen would never be able to bring back such a picture.

The little fat boy nodded. "Yes," he said, quietly. "All right."

A few days later, to Mr. Leslie's complete astonishment, the boy was back again, this time with so excellent a drawing that the editor was very much surprised. There was no need to send the young Thomas on any other difficult quests to bring back proof of his skill. The first had been proof enough.

"What do you make a week where you are now?" asked Mr. Leslie.

"It differs. Sometimes twenty-five cents a week; sometimes six dollars." Thomas looked up into the editor's face soberly.

"Will it average four dollars?"

"Perhaps."

"Very well, then. I will give you four dollars a week," Mr. Leslie promised.

To boys of today, who dream of great wealth as a result of their cartooning, it is interesting to know that the father of American cartoonists began his career in all earnestness on the huge sum of four dollars a week.

Thomas Nast was destined to live and work in very stirring times. By the time he was twenty-one he had made a name for himself with his drawings and was working for

Harper's Weekly. The year he was twenty-one was a very important one in the country's history, for it was 1861, which was the first year of the Civil War. It was natural that his drawings should be of the war, as it was of the most absorbing interest to the whole country. Abraham Lincoln said afterward that "Thomas Nast was our best recruiting officer," for he stirred people into action by the force and power of his cartoons. *Harper's Weekly* circulated in every town, camp, and fort, and so his drawings with their stirring messages reached thousands of people throughout the country. It was a remarkable power to be held by one so young—still a boy! After the war, General Grant was asked what civilian had done most for the cause of the North, and he replied, without hesitation: "Thomas Nast. He did as much as anyone to preserve the Union and bring the war to an end."

During the Revolutionary period, Benjamin Franklin, who, as you remember, had been a printer and the publisher of *Poor Richard's Almanac,* used his own cartoons to express his ideas. In fact, he enjoyed cartooning very much, and felt that he could make himself more clearly understood through them by thousands of people who had learned to read very well. Some of his cartoons had been political and for his country. But cartooning was not an art in those days and Franklin's interest in it was casual and not as intense as Nast's. It was Nast's one entire and absorbing task. But it is interesting to remember that Benjamin Franklin had made cartoons.

Some one has said that in the long history of cartooning

(for people have more or less used cartoons since the days when Egypt was at the height of her power and glory) no cartoonist ever made a more powerful set of cartoons than Thomas Nast used in *Harper's Weekly* against the notorious, vicious "Tweed Ring" in New York City. There were forty-five of these drawings in all. This political ring, headed by a man named "Boss Tweed," was plundering the city, robbing it right and left and dividing the loot with his ring of friends. This was in 1870. Thomas Nast, like all honest people, was horrified by the situation, but with his pen he managed to do what few men could. Week after week, month after month, his stern and relentless pictures appeared. He showed the Tweed Ring no mercy —and they deserved none.

At last Tweed's power was broken and he fled to Europe. However, he had tried to tempt Nast from printing these pictures which were ruining him, by offering him half a million dollars to go to Europe and take up further art studies. Nast was not to be bribed. He was determined that it was Tweed who must leave the country, not he. Nothing that people said or did had half the effect on Tweed that these cartoons had—they haunted him and nearly drove him mad. "I don't care what is done to me, but can't they stop those horrible pictures?" he wailed. Later on, when he was a fugitive in Spain, he was captured because of his resemblance to the Nast pictures. In these remarkable cartoons Nast, single-handed, broke up one of the most vicious groups of crooks the country has known.

Thomas Nast was the creator of some symbols which

are used throughout the United States, and which are so familiar to newspaper readers the country over, that they never stop to realize who it was that first used them. All boys and girls know that the big elephant in newspaper cartoons stands for the Republican party, or the "Grand Old Party." But they do not all know that it was Thomas Nast who first drew the elephant and called him the G.O.P. The G.O.P. elephant first appeared in *Harper's Weekly* in 1874. The symbol which Nast created for the Democratic party, is four years older than the Republican elephant, for Nast drew it for the first time in a copy of *Harper's*, January 15, 1870. The long-eared animal was first called a plain "jackass," but later it became a respectable and more dignified "donkey." It was Nast who invented the "Tammany tiger" which has been used in many political campaigns since. The "labor cap" and the "full dinner pail" are both creations of Thomas Nast, and they, too, are often used symbols in the newspapers.

There was another side of Nast than the relentless and stern avenger of political wrongdoing—a softer, kinder and more gentle side. He was devoted to children everywhere, and he drew for them. He was feared and hated as few men of his day were by unscrupulous politicians, but he was loved by little children. It has often been claimed that he was the first to give children the most dearly beloved symbol of Christmas-giving—Santa Claus. There has been some argument as to whether he was the very first to draw the jolly, fat, bewhiskered gentleman we have come to recognize at once as Santa Claus, but it is true that in

CARTOON *by* Thomas Nast

Harper's Weekly there appeared many drawings of Santa Claus with Nast's name to them, and that his drawings of Santa Claus are identical with the famous poem by Clement Moore, " 'Twas the Night before Christmas." In the long years that Nast cartoons appeared in *Harper's Weekly* there were many Christmas drawings, in fact, the very last drawing he ever made for *Harper's Weekly* was called "The Night before Christmas." What a jolly, happy Santa Claus he put into this picture! It is hard to realize that this lovable, generous old giver of good things was drawn by the same pen as that which had pictured so sternly the greedy face of "Boss Tweed."

For years, wealth poured in on Thomas Nast. He had a beautiful home at Morristown, New Jersey, and in this home he and his wife entertained lavishly. Many famous and prominent people enjoyed their hospitality, among them Mark Twain and General Grant.

Although few men of his day had more power than Thomas Nast, yet his last years were tragically unhappy and miserable. After years of working for *Harper's Weekly* he gave up his connection with them to work independently. From the time he left *Harper's,* misfortune after misfortune befell him, and debts piled upon debts. He had always been lavish and generous with his money, but the time came when he had very little. He did less and less in the way of cartooning. His last work was a painting of Lee's surrender at Appomattox Court House. He painted this picture with a feeling of sympathy for the brilliant general, for he himself had come to know defeat and surrender. After he had painted this picture, a friend met him down in Appomattox Court House in Virginia and asked him "what on earth he was doing down there," to which he replied, "I thought if I came here I might learn to pronounce its name!" It was said half in jest, but it was his last jest. Some of his friends managed to get a government post for him as consul to a South American country. While he was in this tropical country he contracted yellow fever. Far from the land of his adoption—but in her service—he died in exile, from this fever. His death was tragic and lonely, but behind him he had left a splendid record of accomplishments and an honored name. He had placed American cartooning on a high plane, for from his time to this American cartooning is not surpassed by any country in the world.

Thomas Nast is best known for his political cartoons. He lived at a time that needed just the cartoons he had in him to draw. Since his time there have been many other powerful political cartoonists. There have been also brilliant cartoonists who are not interested in politics, but in the everyday life of the people. These cartoons are often drawn in a series, with the story continued from day to day. At one time none of the very best and most dignified newspapers would publish a "comic series." These cartoons, at one time, were cheap, silly, and crude, but today they are as good as they once were bad. Even the most conservative and careful of newspapers run these series in their papers.

The boys of today have come to love and know those very real boys—"Skippy" and the hero of the "Days of

Real Sport." They are just as real and true as Penrod and Tom Sawyer. Every day millions of boys and girls make a wild dash to get the newspaper to continue their acquaintance and friendship with their favorite hero of a "comic series." Millions of grown-up men begin their days, too, with their particular cartoonist—he is as necessary to them as breakfast! The day would be all wrong if they missed one episode in the series! They would be as much out of sorts, if they missed it, as if they had burnt cereal for breakfast or the milkman had failed to leave the milk!

Everyone has his or her favorite cartoonist of everyday life, and it would make a very long story to include them all! We have mentioned only "Skippy," drawn by Crosby, and Clare Briggs's "The Days of Real Sport," because they are for boys and of real boys. Some day these boys will be men, and we will find that they will be still following their old favorite—and a few more.

It was Clare Briggs, the artist who created "The Days of Real Sport," who said "there have been some very wonderful artists who have been famous cartoonists, and it is better to be artistic in cartooning than not!"

And that is the way we began this story. There have been some very famous cartoonists who have been great artists, and America's first great cartoonist and artist was Thomas Nast. It was he who led the way for many splendid and brilliant cartoonists and artists in America!

XI

HOWARD PYLE AND SOME OTHERS

Famous American Illustrators of Children's Books

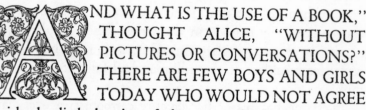ND WHAT IS THE USE OF A BOOK,"
THOUGHT ALICE, "WITHOUT
PICTURES OR CONVERSATIONS?"
THERE ARE FEW BOYS AND GIRLS
TODAY WHO WOULD NOT AGREE
with the little heroine of those remarkable adventures in
Wonderland, and who would not echo after her, "What
is the use of a book without pictures or conversations?"

The strange thing is that for centuries and centuries no
one ever saw any use at all in picture-books for children!
The first picture-book in all history for boys and girls was
not made until 1658. Think of all those long years that
children never had a book of their own, illustrated with
drawings! This first picture-book to be published was called
Obis Pictus, and it was not intended for mere amusement,
as you can imagine, when you know that it was a Latin
school-book! It was certainly not a book that boys and girls
of today would put on their Christmas lists. However, all
honor and credit must go to its author, John Comenius,
who was the first to realize that pictures help children to
enjoy their reading, and that enjoyment makes them remember more vividly what they have read. *Obis Pictus*

is the Latin for the "World in Pictures," and John Comenius wanted to tempt children to enjoy their Latin schoolbook by filling it with many drawings. As he himself said, in his old-fashioned and quaint wording, he desired "to entice witty children, and remove scarecrows from wisdom's garden."

If another Alice, of another day, had spoken her question aloud, say in early Colonial New England, some grown-up would promptly have reminded her "that children should be seen and not heard." Children, in those long-ago days in America, were never asked what they wanted or what they liked, for they were given what was good for them and that was the end of it! What few books there were for children were not intended for entertainment, but to teach some lesson. Although *Obis Pictus* was then in print, it was not a book that any Alice would have taken out into the orchard on a lovely summer day to read under an apple tree for the pure joy of it! She would have been sent to her room to study it, and would have found it a little more enjoyable than her other school-books, because of its pictures.

To teach a lesson! That was the all-important desire of the early writers of children's books. Besides teaching school lessons, these books were planned to teach boys and girls to be very, very good, and to warn them what terrible things would happen to them if they were not. All the first books in New England—and "the all" was very few—taught a moral, and they were very pious and proper morals. It would be very interesting to give a modern boy one of those early books as a present and watch his expression as he read the title and looked the book over. Say, for instance, a book called *Godly Children Their Parents' Joy*, or one called *Young People Warned*. His expression, as he read the titles, would probably be so utterly bewildered, surprised, and dismayed, as to be very funny. One cannot imagine his dashing off with it to read in some undisturbed corner, or his pleading, "Please, mother, let me read just one chapter in *Godly Children Their Parents' Joy*. It's so exciting, that I can't wait until tomorrow to find out what more I can do to be a perfect boy!"

These early books for children, with these stern moral lessons, had no pictures. Not a one! There was nothing about them from first to last to thrill a boy or girl with excitement, or fill him or her with delight, for they were made heavy with fear of what would happen to children who were bad or disobedient. Times, however, change, and everyone, including children, change their ideas with the times in which they live. Artists, too, must change their ideas with the times. Through many centuries, none of the world's great artists had ever illustrated picture-books for children, none of them had ever painted to delight or amuse a child, except on a rare occasion one made a picture to please some royal little prince or princess. Artists, great artists, would have thought it beneath them and wasting their genius and their talents to paint for the young. And no one expected it of them or asked it of them. "Illustrators" were "illustrators," not "artists," for centuries and centuries. However, people began to change their ideas, and the artists, of course, changed theirs. Artists have always used their genius to give to people what they most want. In ancient times the Greeks and Romans wished for beautiful temples and statues of their gods. The Italians who lived in the fourteenth and fifteenth centuries wanted their churches to be made beautiful with holy pictures and statues of saints and biblical heroes. The greatest artists of those centuries used all their wonderful talents to give the Italian people what they wished. Later on, the Dutch desired paintings of people, portraits of themselves and their families, and so we find that their master artists painted portraits. When people began to believe that children should have beauty and joy in their lives, we find that artists were quite ready to give it to them.

It was an Englishman named John Newbery who was the first to make books for boys and girls which had no other use than joy and beauty. This was in 1765, only a few years before the American Revolution. Children in America did not have many picture-books before 1800, as Americans had far too much to do, making themselves into a new nation, to consider anything else. John Newbery made little books bound in bright flowered gilt papers. John Newbery is called "the father of children's literature in England." He wrote and published two hundred books for children and was the first to collect for English children the dearly loved Mother Goose rhymes. His books were filled with many drawings made from woodcuts, and although they were a little crude, they were simple and truthful, and fitted in very closely with the stories. Americans of today fully appreciate all that John Newbery did to make children's books more interesting and beautiful, and in 1922 a prize was offered for the best children's book published each year in America, and it was named for the "father of children's literature," for it is called "The John Newbery Prize."

John Newbery's books were brought to New England by an American named Isaiah Thomas. Isaiah Thomas changed the books somewhat so that they would be more New England than Old England. These books, too, had pictures, but they were written about little girls and boys who were absolutely perfect. You can guess that from their names—"Miss Nancy Careful" or "Miss Betsy All Good." Miss Nancy, as you can imagine from her name, was a careful little girl, and Miss Betsy was nothing short of "all good." Any boys—and, sad to relate, it was always the boys—who were bad were always properly punished, always met with some awful mishap for their wickedness! Little girls were always very, very good, and little boys were always very, very naughty! This was the type of book that New Englanders of these times would think very fitting and proper for their children. You see, even at the beginning of the eighteen hundreds, when the United States was a very new nation, there were practically no children's books that were intended to fill children with pure delight, for they still had to teach a moral.

The Centennial, which celebrated America's first one hundred years of independence, was, as you know, in 1876. What books had the children, who lived in the

United States before that time, really enjoyed? What books with pictures as well as conversations? As we have already said, America had not, up to the time of the Centennial, had many great painters, and practically no sculptors. Once again we must say that there were very good reasons that this was so. It could hardly have been otherwise in a young country, struggling with vastly important problems. Had there been any great illustrators—any illustrators to make children's books interesting and beautiful? Since illustrators of children's books were very new in the history of far older countries, it is not at all surprising to discover that there were none in America before the Centennial. Fortunate boys and girls up to that time had books printed abroad and enjoyed the fascinating illustrations of an Englishman named Cruikshank. Cruikshank was famous for his drawings for Charles Dickens's novels, but he took a keen delight in illustrating books intended only for children. His illustrations very likely were the ones that Alice in Wonderland had enjoyed, because they had appeared just before her time. His illustrations were pure fun. He made all sorts of fairy folks spring to life on a printed page —gnomes, elves, pixies, hobgoblins, genii, and trolls. Never before had this fairy troop been so vividly pictured on the pages of children's books! Cruikshank knew how to make children tingle with excitement, knew how to give them a good laugh. Illustrators of children's books had never before thought that children should be made to laugh. This was in 1824—and how very different are the titles of the books illustrated by Cruikshank from the ones of which we have just read—for instance, *Grimm's Popular Stories, Tom Thumb, The Brownies* and his own fairy book called *The Cruikshank's Fairy*. Alice, and all the boys and girls of today would see "more use" to these books than *Godly Children Their Parents' Joy* or *Miss Betsy All Good*. Times certainly were changing, and illustrators with them.

After Cruikshank came two other Englishmen whose names also began with C—Caldecott and Crane—who delighted children with their drawings. Just looking through a book illustrated by Walter Crane would make any boy or girl feel the glamour and fascination of old legends and fairy stories. His pictures were not of everyday people, but the unreal, strange inhabitants of the fairy world. He illustrated *Hawthorne's Wonder Book, The Yellow Dwarf, Jack and the Beanstalk,* and *Aladdin and his Wonderful Lamp*. Caldecott drew for small children— the "littlest ones"—and his drawings gave joy and delight to very little boys and girls before they could read for themselves. Among the stories that Caldecott illustrated were *The Rhymes of Mother Goose, The House that Jack Built,* and *Hey, Diddle*. His drawings were funny enough to make children laugh with pure glee. When Caldecott died it was said that "the laughter of little children grew less."

Alice in Wonderland was written by Lewis Carroll and illustrated by Sir John Tenniel. It was published in England in 1862. Both the story and the pictures are the most gorgeous nonsense, and never had pictures and story been in such perfect harmony. When one reads of Alice, the

White Rabbit, the Duchess, or the Cheshire Cat, one pictures them just as John Tenniel drew them. Alice herself would never have complained of her own book—for it was just as she wanted a book to be—full of pictures and conversations. Little boys and girls in England and in America, before 1876—loved the happy foolishness and fancy of *Alice in Wonderland* as so many children have from that day to this.

From the beginning of the eighteen hundreds we find books, and the pictures in books for children were becoming happier, brighter, and more inspiring. Artists were beginning to devote their talents to delighting children. Before we speak of America's first famous illustrator of children's books we might mention two other illustrators who made charming books. One was an Englishwoman named Kate Greenaway. Your grandmother will tell you what a rage Kate Greenaway was in her day. Her drawings were very pretty, pale, and dainty. The sturdy little girls of today might think the little girls in Kate Greenaway's story *too* dainty and *too* pale. But in those days it was the style for little girls to be very delicate and sweet. She always pictured her little girls in long dresses to their tiny feet, and on their nicely curled hair were quaint bonnets. People went quite wild over these picturesque costumes, and little girls everywhere were dressed in the "Kate Greenaway" style.

One of the finest illustrators of children's books—for he was called a "prince of illustrators"—was a Frenchman named Boutet de Monvel. Almost everyone, everywhere, who cares about children's illustrations agree that his drawings are very fine, for they are full of life, simple and lovely. His most charming and famous book of illustrations is of France's most beloved heroine Joan of Arc.

America's first great illustrator of children's books, Howard Pyle, was born in Wilmington, Delaware, in 1853. He was twenty-four years old at the time of the Centennial in Philadelphia, but up to that time he had not made any great success of his drawing. He had had to go into business and content himself with drawing in his leisure time, after hours in the evening or on holidays. Pyle was intensely patriotic, believed with his whole heart in the future of American artists and illustrators. His entire school training was in America, as well as his art training, for he did not believe in American artists going abroad to study. His art training had been at the Art Students' League in New York City. Throughout his long, busy years of working to make American illustrations finer and worthy to stand beside those of Europe, no man had more influence than he. He was a pioneer, giving to America and American children something new, something of their very own. Although the illustrators of today are not working in the same manner and style as Howard Pyle, we must give him all credit and honor and glory for being the first American artist to devote his talents and his labors to making children's books beautiful. Not only did he illustrate books for children, but he wrote a great many of the stories for which he made paintings and drawings. He inspired other artists and authors to give the best they had in them to children's books. He made people respect illustrators as they never had before.

America had been a little slow, perhaps, in giving to her children beautiful books, but once she got well started under Howard Pyle her interest in them grew with each passing year, until today no country cares more, gives more, or pays more for fine and beautiful books for children. Howard Pyle became a noted art-teacher, for he felt in teaching he could inspire others to follow the ideals in which he so ardently believed. America had already had some splendid art-teachers—William M. Chase and Kenyon Cox—but it was Howard Pyle who used his powers as a teacher to encourage illustrators and to inspire them to finer work. He taught in the Drexel Institute in Philadelphia, the Art Students' League in New York City, and his own school in Wilmington, Delaware. In his own school he did not charge tuition; he was happy and content to take pupils free who were interested in illustrating. He inspired all who came under him with his intense belief in the future of art and illustrating in America. A large number of his pupils have become famous illustrators of children's books. Perhaps there are none more famous than Maxfield Parrish or Jessie Wilcox Smith. Maxfield Parrish is noted for the radiance of his colors—most particularly an intense and brilliant blue. He illustrated, among others, *Arabian Nights* and the *Poems of Childhood,* by Eugene Field. In thousands of kindergartens and first grades his beautiful "Wynken, Blynken, and Nod" delighted little children, from its place on the wall. Jessie Wilcox Smith's charming Mother Goose pictures are in quite as many kindergartens, and her paintings of little boys and girls on the covers of *Good Housekeeping Magazine* are known far and wide over the United States. These are only two of countless artists who were inspired by Howard Pyle. He was, as we have said, absolutely devoted to America and to American illustrators, and he never left America until late in his life. In 1910 he went to Italy, the country that most artists hope to see some day before they die. By a strange turn of fate, it was in this country that Howard Pyle died a year later, in 1911, in the glorious city of Florence.

Among the long list of books illustrated by Howard Pyle, including *Men of Iron, The Wonder Clock, The Merry Adventures of Robin Hood, The Story of King Arthur and Knights, Otto of the Silver Hand,* none is more beloved than his *Book of Pirates.* Boys, and girls, too, relish his very real and vivid "pirates." When one thinks of story-book pirates one must think of Howard Pyle's famous and romantic pirates. Pyle not only painted his illustrations in strong, bright colors, but he made some fine, powerful drawings in black and white. Until after the World War, most of the illustrators in America painted in the same fashion as Howard Pyle. Even today he still has many followers.

Another famous illustrator, who lived and worked at the same time as Howard Pyle, was Frederic Remington. Remington, like Howard Pyle, was thoroughly American, for all his training and schooling was received in the United States. Frederic Remington loved the West, and in his day

Buried Treasure *by* Howard Pyle

it was still the "wild West." His pictures are filled with Indians, cowboys, and ponies, and no other illustrator made them seem so real.

The World War was a turning-point in the story of American illustrators. During those long, grim, cruel years of war, when the whole world was torn with terrible misery, little children, the world over, had had a black shadow cast over their childhood. When the war was ended and peace had come again, grown-up people were eager to think of happier things than bloodshed. Perhaps because their own lives had been saddened, they were determined that their children's should not be. They were glad to think of their children, and anxious to give them as much as possible of what was bright and beautiful, so that they might grow up and make the world brighter and more beautiful. So many lovely things had been destroyed in the war, and it is the young people who must some day replace them. It was determined that the young lives of today should be flooded with joy and beauty. America's books for children after the World War were quite different from what they had ever been before in her history. No country in the world today is giving so much attention to its youth as America. Surely it is the golden age of childhood, even to the littlest ones.

The great publishing-houses that make books, shortly after the war decided that more attention should be given to children's books, so that from cover to cover they should be finer and more beautiful. They made special departments for boys' and girls' books, and these boys' and girls' books were given the same attention and thought as the books of grown-ups had been given in the past. The libraries built more and more rooms just for children—bright sunny rooms, gay with brilliant pictures—and placed upon the children's shelves the finest and very best of books for the little folks to enjoy to their hearts' content. Once a year it was planned that there should be a "Children's Book Week," so that the whole country over should think of the importance of fine books for children. During the Great War we heard of all sorts of "weeks"—"meatless" and "heatless," for instance—weeks in which people were to give up something to help their country at war. It was the first time people had ever heard of "this week" or "that week." Although we still have a few "weeks" celebrated each year, as "thrift week," or "fire-prevention week," none gives a happier promise than "Children's Book Week." For if children, from the time they are very, very little, are given beautiful things, surely they will grow up to love beauty so that they will do everything to make their country a more wonderful land.

Artists, of course, were overjoyed and eager to help bring beauty into the lives of children, as we have found that artists are always ready to use their genius in giving to people what they want most in the way of beauty. Each year, since the war, artists have been outdoing themselves in an endeavor to do finer work. This story of American illustrators of children's books is only just begun, for it is very certain that more and more artists are going to devote their lives to making children's books beautiful.

Jessie Wilcox Smith's colored posters for children were first put into book form in 1919—the year after the Armistice. Since then, children's colored picture-books have come thick and fast. Besides the American artists who are working for children, several splendid foreign artists have come to America to make their homes and are painting and drawing for American children. Two of the most famous of these are Boris Artzybasheff and Willy Pogany. Boris Artzybasheff (a long name for children's tongues, but his drawings are a delight to their eyes) fled from Russia after two revolutions, during which his home was burned down. Because of this misfortune, children in America are more fortunate, for no artist has made stronger and more beautiful drawings in black and white than Boris Artzybasheff. His drawings, besides illustrating their story, make a beautiful pattern and design upon the page. Willy Pogany is a Hungarian who paints somewhat like our Maxfield Parrish. He has illustrated *The Gingerbread Man,* and some of the fascinating stories written by Padraic Colum.

What American artists have made boys' books more wonderful by their illustrations—besides Howard Pyle and Frederic Remington? N. C. Wyeth has illustrated Cooper's *The Deerslayer* and *The Last of the Mohicans* and Robert Louis Stevenson's *Kidnapped* and *Treasure Island,* and many others, and has succeeded in making them even more vivid and wonderful.

Perhaps no American artist today has made more virile books for boys than James G. Daugherty. "Jimmy" Daugherty was born in North Carolina, and when he was only a very little fellow his family moved to southern Ohio. What wonderful times he had along the Ohio River. He was tempted many times to "play hooky" from the country school, to go swimming and trout-fishing. He was fascinated by water always, and loved to play around the docks and waterfronts. When he was in his " 'teens" his family moved again, this time to Washington, D. C. His father was a very cultured gentleman and it was he who encouraged "Jimmy" in his interest in art, and suggested that he go to the Corcoran Art Gallery in Washington and study its great paintings. There were many fine art schools in Washington, and "Jimmy" had an excellent opportunity to have some good art training. It is no wonder that he should paint spirited, exciting, and powerful pictures, for he had always been a "very regular boy" himself and had loved all the things real boys love. Daugherty believed very deeply in America's future as an artistic nation, and he believed that beautiful books were going to be an important part of her art. Certainly his illustrations for Stewart Edward White's *Daniel Boone* is an addition of great worth to the American art of book-making! Daugherty has poured into the paintings and illustrations of this book all the pioneer spirit that was much a part of him. His illustrations are as vivid, rugged, and bold as the times he pictured. From cover to cover, Daugherty's *Daniel Boone* is a work of art. His drawings for Sandburg's *Lincoln Grows Up* and for *The Knickerbocker's History of New York* have also this vital American spirit. He had practiced what he preached—

America could produce books that were works of art, books that would live!

And who has brought the fairy folk dancing across the pages of our books today? Who has made these lovely glamorous folk real? What artist has enchanted us by pen and brush, touched us as if by a wand, so that we feel the magic of the fairy world? Not one artist, but several.

Two women artists, Dorothy Lathrop and Elizabeth MacKinstry, have each held a magic wand in their hands (a wand that has all the appearance of a pen or a brush!) and have transformed a white sheet of paper into a fairy realm. Dorothy Lathrop has illustrated *Silver Horn, Down-a-down-Derry* and *Mopsa the Fairy;* and Elizabeth Mac-Kinstry *Puck in Pasture.* This is Elizabeth MacKinstry's own book of a gypsy camp; story as well as illustrations are hers. She has also made entrancing illustrations for the French fairy tales by Madame D'Aulnoy, *The White Cat.* These two artists do not confine themselves to fantasy alone, for Dorothy Lathrop's illustrations for *Hitty* and Elizabeth MacKinstry's for *The Night before Christmas* are high-water marks in illustrated art.

The list of American illustrators of children's books is becoming a long one and is growing longer every year. New names came thick and fast in the first dozen years after the Great War—new artists who were painting in a new way; they no longer followed the methods and manners of How-ard Pyle. We might almost say that there had been a "Howard Pyle school of illustration," for so many artists had followed his style. After the war there was a "new" school of illustration, and artists who illustrated children's books worked in a very new way. They thought more of making their work a part of the beautiful design of the book—planning to have their paintings or drawings in perfect and beautiful harmony with the shape and character of the book,—than making their illustrations exact and real. How often have we read an author's description of a hero or heroine, only to turn to the illustration and find that the artist had painted his own exact impression of the character, and not ours, nor perhaps even the author's idea! The artists after the Great War did not try to be so exact and so real. They said to themselves, "We shall make pictures that will delight the eye, beautiful in design and color; we will not try to put down dot for dot the author's description of a character or we may fail and disappoint; but we will make illustrations so lovely and beautiful that as a child turns over the pages of his precious new book he will be as eager to read it as a singer is ready to burst into song at the sound of music! We will be the music for the author's song of words! In the old way sometimes the music was so loud that it drowned out the song. Illustrations to be in perfect harmony with the author's story should be only what a musical accompaniment is to a song.

Among the long list of new American illustrators of children's books in the first twelve years after the Great War let us mention a dozen (so it will be easier to remember—a dozen years—a dozen artists). We have already mentioned five—Jessie Wilcox Smith, N. C. Wyeth, James G.

Daugherty, Dorothy Lathrop, and Elizabeth MacKinstry —so let us complete the dozen, for splendid work has also been done by Pamela Bianco, Peggy Bacon, Erick Berry, Maginal Wright Barney, Lois Lenski, Henry A. Pitz, and the Petershams (the Petershams are two people)—so making this dozen a baker's dozen, which, after all, is a very proper and generous number for children. And one more for good measure—Tony Sarg! A baker's dozen and one more for good measure of American illustrators of children's books in a dozen years.

While this story is being written the baker's dozen and one for good measure are spending happy hours busily engaged in making new and more beautiful books for children. Not only the baker's dozen and one more for good measure, but just as many more again! We might begin another baker's dozen with the name of Wanda Gag, who has given us her delightful *Millions of Cats*. Each year there will be new names—artists now unknown, who will be added to the bright and shining list of illustrators of children's books.

As we have said, this story of American illustrators is just begun (which is a funny place to end a tale). It is a story to be lived, not read, and is being lived by millions of happy, eager boys and girls who are reveling in their good fortune in having famous artists working for them. No little prince or princess of long ago is so happy or fortunate as they are! What a golden future there is in store for children in America, for it is certain that the children of today, who have been given such beautiful books, will grow up and give more beautiful books to their own children.

We must once again give all credit to Howard Pyle, who was the first to give American children books which from cover to cover were beautiful, for he blazed a new trail into a happy, glorious realm—a land of golden treasure and promise for millions of children!

BIBLIOGRAPHY

Briggs, Clare, *How to Draw Cartoons*.
Brinton, Christian, *Modern Artists*.
Chaffin, Charles, *American Masters of Painting*.
Charteris, Hon. Evan, *John Singer Sargent*.
Cooper, Anice Page, *Authors and Others*.
Cortissoz, Royal, *American Artists*.
Downs, William Howe, { *The Life and Works of Winslow Homer*. *John Singer Sargent*.
Garderner, Helen, *Art Through the Ages*.
Gardner and Ramsey, *A Handbook of Children's Literature*.
Hubbard, Elbert, *Little Journeys*.
Inness, George, Jr., *Life and Letters of George Inness*.
Isham, Samuel, *The History of American Painting*.
Jackson, Rilla Evelyn, *American Arts*.
Lucas, E. V., *Edwin Austin Abbey*.
Mahoney, Bertha, and Whitney, Elinor, *Realms of Gold*.
Maurice, Arthur Barlett and Frederick Taber Cooper, *The History of the Nineteenth Century in Caricature*.
McSpadden, Joseph Walker, { *Famous Painters of America*. *Famous Sculptors of America*.
Moore, Anne Carroll, *The Three Owls*.
Pach, Walter, *Ananias, the False Artist*.
Parks, Laurence, *Gilbert Stuart*.
Parton, James, *Caricature*.
Payne, Albert Bigelow, *Thomas Nast*.
Pennell, Elizabeth Robbins, *Life and Letters of Joseph Pennell*.

227

Bibliography

Pennell, E. R. and J., *The Life of James McNeill Whistler*.
Pennell, Joseph, *Etchers and Etching*.
Saint Gaudens, Homer, *Life and Letters of Augustus Saint Gaudens*.
Taft, Lorado, *The History of American Sculptors*.
Tuckerman, Henry Theodore, *Eminent American Painters*.
Van Dyke, John Charles, *American Painting*.
Weitenkampf, Frank, *American Graphic Art*.